Jack Kerouac and the Traditions of Classic and Modern Haiku

Jack Kerouac and the Traditions of Classic and Modern Haiku

Yoshinobu Hakutani

LEXINGTON BOOKS
Lanham • Boulder • New York • London

Published by Lexington Books
An imprint of The Rowman & Littlefield Publishing Group, Inc.
4501 Forbes Boulevard, Suite 200, Lanham, Maryland 20706
www.rowman.com

6 Tinworth Street, London SE11 5AL, United Kingdom

British Library Cataloguing in Publication Information Available

Library of Congress Cataloging-in-Publication Data Available

Library of Congress Control Number: 2018961616

ISBN: 978-1-4985-5827-3 (cloth : alk paper)
ISBN: 978-1-4985-5828-0 (electronic)

♾™ The paper used in this publication meets the minimum requirements of American National Standard for Information Sciences—Permanence of Paper for Printed Library Materials, ANSI/NISO Z39.48-1992.

Printed in the United States of America

Text Permission

Chapter 3 adapted from "Yone Noguchi's Poetry: From Whitman to Zen." *Comparative Literature Studies*, Vol 22(1). 1985. 67–79.

"A big fat lake," "A bird hanging," "A bird on," "A bottle of wine," "A quiet Autumn night," "After the shower," "Ah, the crickets," "All these sages," "Am I a flower," "April mist," "Bee, why are you," "Birds chirp," "Content, the top t" "Dawn-crows cawing," "Desk cluttered," "Desolation, desolation," "Dusk the blizzard," "Everywhere beyond,." "Following each other," "Frozen," "Grow worms," "Greyhound bus," "Hand in hand in a red valley," "High noon," "Hot coffee," "I close my eyes," "I called Dipankara," "I called Hanshan," "I made raspberry jello," "I said a joke," "Ignoring my bread," "In back of the supermarket," "In enormous blizzard," "In my medicine cabinet," "In the sun," "Jack reads his book," "Late afternoon," "Lay the pencil," "Loves his own belly," "Looking for my cat," "May grass," "Mist falling," "No telegram today," "O Sebastian, where are thou?," "On desolation," "Or, walking the same or different," "Perfect moonlit night," "Quietly pouring coffee," "Rainy night," "Reading the sutra," "Reflected upside-down," "Rig rig rig," "River wonderland," "Sex shaking to breed," "Shall I heed God's commandment?," "Shall I say no?," "Shooting star! no," "Spring day," "Spring evening," "Sunday," "Take up a cup of water," 'The angel's hair," "The backyard I tried to draw," "The crickets crying," "The bottom of

To the Memory of
MICHIKO HAKUTANI

Contents

Acknowledgments

For this study of Jack Kerouac's published haiku, I would like to acknowledge quoting many of the haiku from *Book of Haikus* by Jack Kerouac, edited and with an Introduction by Regina Weinreich, (New York: Penguin Books, 2003).

The Kent State University Research Council granted a research leave for this project. Over the years the Council has also provided several travel grants for my study of haiku. I am grateful for their support.

I am also indebted to many writers and sources, as acknowledged in the notes and works cited. I would like to thank, in particular, the late Robert L. Tener and the late Michiko Hakutani for their insights and inspirations.

I am grateful to the anonymous reviewers for Lexington Books, who read part or all of the manuscript and offered useful, constructive suggestions. I would also like to thank Ben Tjoelker of Netherlands for offering his illustration of Jack Kerouac for the book cover, Toru Kiuchi for constructing indexes, and my son Yoshiki Hakutani for his technical support.

I have used in modified form my previously published essays: "Yone Noguchi's Poetry: From Whitman to Zen" (*Comparative Literature Studies*, 1985); "Ezra Pound, Yone Noguchi, and Imagism" (*Modern Philology*, 1992); "Cross-Cultural Poetics: Sonia Sanchez's *Like the Singing Coming off the Drums*" and "James Emanuel's Jazz Haiku and African American Individualism" in *Cross-Cultural Visions in African American Modernism: From Spatial Narrative to Jazz Haiku* (Ohio State University Press, 2006); and "Richard Wright's Haiku, Zen, and the African 'Primal Outlook upon Life'" (*Modern Philology*, 2007).

Introduction

One of the most popular East–West artistic, cultural, and literary exchanges that have taken place in modern and postmodern times was reading and writing of haiku in the West. The end of World War II provoked an outpouring of interest in Japanese haiku. British writers in Tokyo began to renew Western interest in haiku. The most important of these writers were Harold G. Henderson and R. H. Blyth. Their interest in haiku and subsequent books and translations made haiku a viable literary art form for Western poets.

John Gould Fletcher also introduced the West to Kenneth Yasuda's *A Pepper-Pod*, a translation of Japanese haiku with selections of original haiku written in English in 1946. Gary Snyder wrote haiku in his diary, published in 1952 under the title *Earth House Hold*. Allen Ginsberg read Blyth's work on haiku and started to write haiku himself. An entry in his journal reads, "Haiku composed in the backyard cottage at . . . Berkeley 1955, while reading R. H. Blyth's 4 volumes *Haiku*." In 1958 Harold G. Henderson's revised 1930 work, retitled *An Introduction to Haiku*, appeared in America and generated more interest in haiku. In fact, hundreds of Americans, some Canadians and British, began to write haiku (Higginson, *Haiku Handbook* 63–64).

Among the writers who tried their hand at composing haiku in English, the two American novelists, Richard Wright (1908–60) and Jack Kerouac (1922–69), distinguished themselves as haiku poets. In the last eighteen months of his life Wright, the revolutionary American writer known for *Native Son* (1940) and *Black Boy* (1945), wrote over 4,000 haiku. After his death, the Wright estate deposited, in Yale's Beinecke Rare Book and Manuscript Library, the two manuscripts: "This Other World: Projections in the Haiku Manner" and "Four Thousand Haiku." The first manuscript was published as *Haiku: This Other World*, ed. Yoshinobu Hakutani and Robert L. Tener (Arcade, 1998 / rept. Random House, 2000, rept. Arcade/Sky Horse,

2012, under the title, *Haiku: The Last Poems of an American Icon*). This edition constitutes Wright's own selection of 817 out of about four thousand haiku Wright wrote in the last eighteen months of his life.

On the other hand, Jack Kerouac, who captured a huge audience when his novel, *On the Road*, appeared in 1957, also wrote numerous haiku throughout his career and played a central role in the literary movement he named the Beat Generation. His other novel *The Dharma Bums* (1958) gave an intimate biographical account of himself in search of the truths in life. In San Francisco he met Gary Snyder and the two Dharma bums explored the thoughts and practices of Buddhism. Through his friendship with such Beat poets as Allen Ginsberg (1926–97) and Gary Snyder (1930–), as well as through his studies of Buddhism and Zen philosophy, Kerouac firmly established his poetics.

Kerouac's motive for writing haiku coincided with the movement of the Beat Generation. The unrestrained story of Kerouac and Snyder on the West Coast also coincided with the birth of the San Francisco Poetry Renaissance. Kerouac called the event "the whole gang of howling poets" gathered at Gallery Six on October 13, 1955. In the beginning of *The Dharma Bums*, Kerouac described the poetry reading:

> Everyone was there. It was a mad night. And I was the one who got things jumping by going around collecting dimes and quarters from the rather stiff audience standing around in the gallery and coming back with three huge gallon jugs of California Burgundy and getting them all piffed so that by eleven o'clock when Alvah Goldbook [Allen Ginsberg] was reading his, wailing his poem "Wail" [Howl] drunk with arms outspread everybody was yelling "Go! Go! Go!" (like a jam session) and old Rheinhold Cacoethes the father of the Frisco poetry scene was wiping his tears in gladness. Japhy [Gary Snyder] himself read his fine poems about Coyote the God of the North American Plateau Indians (I think), at least the God of the Northwest Indians, Kwakiutl and what-all. "Fuck you! sang Coyote, and ran away!" read Japhy to the distinguished audience, making them all howl with joy, it was so pure, fuck being a dirty word that comes out clean. And he had his tender lyrical lines, like the ones about bears eating berries, showing his love of animals, and great mystery lines about oxen on the Mongolian road showing his knowledge of Oriental literature even on to Hsuan Tsung the great Chinese monk who walked from China to Tibet, Lanchow to Kashgar and Mongolia carrying a stick of incense in his hand. (13–14)

Not only did this inaugural meeting of the Beat Generation feature the three well-known writers Kerouac, Snyder, and Ginsberg (1926–1997), their subsequent interactions among them revealed their backgrounds and worldviews. Snyder, born in San Francisco, followed Ginsberg's first reading of *Howl* at this gathering with his own lyrical poems, as mentioned above. Later in *The Dharma Bums* Snyder observed, "East'll meet West anyway. Think what a great world revolution will take place when East meets West finally, and it'll be guys like us that can start the thing. Think of millions of guys all over the world with rucksacks on their backs tramping around the back country and hitchhiking and bringing the word down to everybody." Kerouac responded by referring to a Christian tradition he remembered as he grew up a Catholic in a French-Canadian family in Massachusetts: "That's a lot like the early days of the Crusades, Walter the Penniless and Peter the Hermit leading ragged bands of believers to the Holy Land." Snyder, admonishing Kerouac against believing in his Western legacy, said, "Yeah but that was all such European gloom and crap, I want my Dharma Bums to have springtime in their hearts when the blooms are girling and the birds are dropping little fresh turds surprising cats who wanted to eat them a moment ago" (*Dharma Bums* 60).

Discussing Buddhism and, in particular, Zen philosophy with Snyder, as well as reading books on Buddhism in the local libraries, Kerouac realized that Buddhism, rather than denying suffering and death, confronted both. For him, Buddhism taught one to transcend the origin of suffering and death: desire and ignorance. Most impressively, Buddhism taught Kerouac that the phenomenal world was like a dream and an illusion and that happiness consisted in achieving that strange vision in the mind—enlightenment. *The Dharma Bums* also informs that while Snyder was continuously fascinated with Zen, Kerouac was inspired by Mahayana Buddhism. To Kerouac, Zen, which teaches spontaneous, realistic action for human beings, compromises with active, worldly existence. Consequently, Zen admonished against existing in a world of temptation and evil. On the contrary, Kerouac was impressed with Mahayama Buddhism, for one's goal of life is to achieve Buddhahood, a celestial state of enlightenment and acceptance of all forms of life.

The genesis of the Beat movement goes back to the meeting of Kerouac and Ginsberg at Columbia University in the early 1940s. Kerouac and Ginsberg, who grew up in New Jersey of Russian Jewish immigrant parents, also shared their literary interests with William Burroughs (1914–1997), who hailed from Missouri. During this period Kerouac, immersed with American transcendentalism, read Emerson, Thoreau, and Whitman. Kerouac was influenced by Emerson's concept of self-reliance as he learned of Whitman's singular, stubborn independence and refusal to subscribe to society's materialistic, commercial demands. At the same time it was Thoreau's writings, such as *Walden, A Week on the Concord and Merrimack Rivers*, and "Civil Disobedience" that introduced Kerouac to Confucianism and Buddhism.[1]

Learning about Buddhism from Thoreau, Kerouac became seriously interested in studying its philosophy. His study of Buddhism, then, led to writing *The Dharma Bums*. For Kerouac, Mahayana Buddhism served to change the state of defeat in the world that the Beat movement represented to the beatific acceptance of life the Buddhist texts described. For Gary Snyder, Zen Buddhism transformed the Beats to the Zen Lunatics.

For Kerouac, and for the Beat Generation, the Zen perspective made art conform to life itself. A Zen-inspired poet must see whatever happens in life—order and disorder, permanence and change. This Zen principle partly accounts for Kerouac's rejection of the idea of revision.[2] Kerouac's composition of haiku reflects the spontaneous mode of writing that he acquired from classic haiku he read in Blyth's book. While abiding by the principles and techniques of haiku shown by Blyth, Kerouac realized that an English haiku cannot be composed in seventeen syllables as in Japanese. "Western languages," Kerouac noted, "cannot adapt themselves to the fluid syllabic Japanese. I propose that the 'Western Haiku' simply say a lot in three short lines in any Western language." "Above all," he emphasized, "a Haiku must be very simple and free of all poetic trickery and makes a little picture and yet be as airy and graceful as a Vivaldi Pastorella." He presented, as examples, three haiku by Basho, Buson, and Issa, saying they are "simpler and prettier than any Haiku I could ever write in any language" (Tonkinson 74):

> A day of quiet gladness,—
> Mount Fuji is veiled
> In misty rain.
>
> > (Basho) (1644–1694)

> The nightingale is singing,
> Its small mouth
> Open.
>
> > (Buson) (1715–1783)

> She has put the child to sleep,
> And now washes the clothes:
> The summer moon.
>
> > (Issa) (1763–1827)

In each of the haiku two images are juxtaposed: the veiled Mount Fuji and the misty rain in Basho's haiku, the singing nightingale and its open mouth in Buson's, and the mother having put her child to sleep and washing the clothes and the summer moon in Issa's. Kerouac said in his *Paris Review* interview, "A sentence that's short and sweet with a sudden jump of thought is a kind of haiku, and there's a lot of freedom and fun in surprising yourself with that, let the mind willy-nilly jump from the branch to the bird" (Weinreich, *Book of Haikus* xxiv-xxv).

As Kerouac's *Book of Haikus* indicates, Kerouac continuously wrote haiku to render the Beats's worldview. "For a new generation of poets," Weinreich has observed, "Kerouac ended up breaking ground at a pioneering stage of an American haiku movement" (*Book of Haikus* xv). Allen Ginsberg celebrated Kerouac's haiku:

> Kerouac has the one sign of being a great poet, which is he's the only one in the United States who knows how to write haikus. The only one who's written any good haikus. And everybody's been writing haikus. There are all these dreary haikus written by people who think for weeks trying to write a haiku, and finally come up with some dull little thing or something. Whereas Kerouac thinks in haikus, every time he writes anything—talks that way and thinks that way. So it's just natural for him. It's something Snyder noticed. Snyder has to labor for years in a Zen monastery to produce one haiku about shitting off a log! And actually does get one or two good ones. Snyder was always astounded by Kerouac's facility. (Lynch 123–24)

There were, however, some poets who were not enthusiastic about Kerouac's haiku. Lawrence Ferlinghetti, who was associated with the Beat writers and the San Francisco Renaissance poets and who, founding his own press, published his friend Allen Ginsberg's work, said that Kerouac "was a better novel writer than a poem writer" (Gifford and Lee 271).

As Kerouac tried his hand at composing haiku, he was always reminded of the theory of haiku he learned from Blyth's book. Blyth showed throughout the volumes that much of classic haiku is based on the Eastern philosophies: Buddhist ontology, Zen, and Confucianism. Kerouac was especially impressed with the Buddhist worldview that both humans and nonhumans possess souls and that the soul transmigrates between humans and nonhumans. Buddhists believe in reincarnation: once a human dies the soul one possessed will transmigrate to the soul of a nonhuman. Some of Kerouac's haiku express compassion for animals, birds, and insects as do some of the famous classic haiku. Kobayashi Issa (1762–1826), a Buddhist priest as well as an influential haiku poet in Japanese history, expressed his compassion for a fly:

You dare not strike him!
The fly is praying with hands
And praying with feet.[3]

(Issa)

[*Yare utsu na*
Hai ga te wo suru
Ashi wo suru]

Kerouac, fascinated by the Buddhist doctrine of mercy and compassion, wrote the following haiku:

Shall I say no?
    —fly rubbing
Its back legs

(Kerouac, Book of Haikus 78)

This haiku suggests that Kerouac wrote it in praise of Issa's haiku. Interestingly, Kerouac wrote another haiku on a fly:

Shall I break God's commandment?
    Little fly
Rubbing its back legs

(Kerouac, Book of Haikus 109)

By invoking God's Commandment, Kerouac is conflating the Christian teaching with the Buddhist doctrine of mercy, which his other haiku "Shall I Say No?" expresses. On the other hand, critical of the Christian doctrine of compassion, which concerns only humans, Kerouac wrote this haiku:

Woke up groaning
    With a dream of a priest
Eating chicken necks

(Book of Haikus 31)

Kerouac betrays a nightmare a Christian-converted Buddhist would have. This haiku suggests Kerouac's view of Christians' cruelty to animals.

    Kerouac also learned from Blyth how to express and depict the Zen state of mind. "What Bashō means," Blyth remarks, "is something that belongs to Zen, namely, that we must not wish to do something clever, write a fine poem, but do it as naturally, as freely, as unselfconsciously as a child does everything" (Blyth, *Haiku* 217). Blyth further quotes another haiku by Basho and one by Issa to illustrate the simplicity of haiku:

    You light the fire;
I'll show you something nice,—
    A great ball of snow!

(Basho)

I could eat it!—
This snow that falls
So softly, so softly.

(Issa)

Both haiku are depictions of the simple, natural phenomena in nature that represent the Zen state of mind, which suppresses or minimizes human subjectivity. But Basho's haiku expresses some subjectivity of aesthetics as does Issa's more subjectivity of desire.

Following the principle of simplicity and naturalness, Kerouac wrote numerous haiku, such as the following:

Chipmunk went in
      —butterfly
Came out

(*Book of Haikus* 95)

Sunday—
      The sky is blue,
The flowers are red

(*Book of Haikus* 103)

The little white cat
      Walks in the grass
With his tail up in the air

(*Book of Haikus* 115)

The wind sent
      A leaf on
The robin's back

(*Book of Haikus* 175)

Another way to express and depict the Zen state of mind for Kerouac was to construct the image of *mu*, nothingness. In Zen, the state of nothingness is not equated with the void but represents the absence of human subjectivity, self-centeredness. In practical terms, achieving such a concept enables the believer to empty the mind of egotism and selfishness. Blyth calls this state of mind "a state of absolute spiritual poverty in which, having nothing, we possess all" (*Haiku* 162). Kerouac wrote many haiku with the image of *mu*, such as the following:

There is no deep
        turning-about
in the Void

(Book of Haikus 75)

Everywhere beyond
        the Truth,
Empty space blue

(Book of Haikus 86)

There's nothing there
        because
I don't care

(Book of Haikus 87)

I called—Dipankara
        instructed me
By saying nothing

(Book of Haikus 93)

The second haiku, "Everywhere Beyond," depicts and expresses not only the state of *mu*, but also the state of eternity.

Kerouac also learned from Blyth that classic haiku poets like Basho were influenced by Confucianism. For Confucias, God is not a living being like a human being: God is a concept that originated from a human being. The individual in society must formulate this concept by apprehending the ways of nature in heaven and on earth. One must be conscious of the supremacy of heaven over earth and humans. Some of Kerouac's haiku express this worldview, for example:

Reflected upsidedown,
        in the sunset lake, pines
Pointing to infinity

(Book of Haikus 101)

This haiku focuses on an image of the universe that makes human existence infinitesimal in contrast to an infinite space that represents the universe.

Kerouac's haiku, "The Backyard I Tried to Draw," has an affinity with Basho's, "The Mountains and Gardens Also Move," in its expression of the Confucian worldview:

The backyard I tried to draw
    —It still looks
The same

(Kerouac, Book of Haikus 117)

    The mountains and garden also move;
The summer drawing-room
    Includes them.

(Basho, Blyth, Haiku 38)

The garden in Basho's haiku represents a space shared by human beings and earth. So does the backyard in Kerouac's haiku. Both images suggest that despite the human creation of the space, they still belong to earth, a permanent space under heaven.

The following haiku by Kerouac also describe the control the universe has over the earth and humanity:

Following each other,
    my cats stop
When it thunders

(Kerouac, Book of Haikus 27)

The summer chair
    rocking by itself
In the blizzard

(Kerouac, Book of Haikus 36)

In these haiku, the phenomena above the earth and human beings have control over them. The first haiku, "Following Each Other," captures the moment when the thunderstorm halts the cats' movement. In the second haiku, "The Summer Chair," the blizzard rather than a human being is rocking the chair. Another haiku on the same subject, "In the sun / the butterfly wings / Like a church window" (62), suggests that human law must follow the law of the universe.

For the technique of haiku composition, and the use of imagery in particular, Kerouac relied on Snyder's advice. Kerouac, while hiking in the mountains with Snyder, said, "Walking in this country you could understand the perfect gems of haikus the Oriental poets had written, never getting drunk in the mountains or anything but just going along as fresh as children writing down what they saw without literary devices of fanciness of expression. We made up haikus as we climbed, winding up and up now on the slopes of brush" (*Dhama Bums* 59). Snyder responded, "A real haiku's gotta be as simple as porridge and yet make you see the real thing, like the greatest haiku of them all probably is the one that goes 'The sparrow hops along the veranda, with wet feet.' By Shiki.[4] You see the wet footprints like a vision in your mind and yet in those few words you also see all the rain that's been falling that day and almost smell the wet pine needles'" (*Dharma Bums* 59).

Kerouac and Snyder both emphasized that haiku must be simple, the principle that Blyth considers a salient characteristic of haiku. As an example Blyth quotes a haiku Basho composed on his travels:

> The Rose of Sharon
> By the roadside,
>> Was eaten by the horse.
>
>   (Basho, Blyth, *Haiku* 217)

Kerouac, while he was traveling on the road for writing *On the Road*, composed in his mind many haiku that simply depict what he saw. Under the heading "Road Haiku," such haiku were included among the seventy-five haiku collected as Road Haiku / Summer. For example, the following haiku simply depict some of the scenes Kerouac saw on the road:

> The jazz trombone,
>> The moving curtain,
> —Spring rain
>
>   (*Book of Haikus* 114)

> Greyhound bus,
>> flowing all night,
> Virginia
>
>   (*Book of Haikus* 114)

> Loves his own belly
>> The way I love my life,
> The white cat
>
>   (*Book of Haikus* 115)

The little white cat
    Walks in the grass
With his tail up in the air

                                    (*Book of Haikus* 115)

    In a series of discussion on Pound's theory of imagism Kerouac had with Snyder and Ginsberg, Kerouac became aware that American modernist poets like Snyder and Ginsberg were enthusiastic about Pound's theory. Snyder told Kerouac and Ginsberg that Pound is Snyder's favorite poet. Kerouac, however, had no interest in Pound, let alone his theory of imagism. One of the discussions by the three was recorded in the beginning of *The Dharma Bums*:

Alva [Ginsberg]: What are all these strange books here? Hm, Pound, do you like Pound?
Japhy [Snyder]: Except for the fact that that old fartface flubbed up the name of Li Po by calling him by his Japanese name and all such famous twaddle, he was all right—in fact he's my favorite poet.
Ray [Kerouac]: Pound? Who wants to make a favorite poet out of that pretentious nut?

                                    (*Dharma Bums* 26)

    As late as the 1950s, Pound's theory of imagism, the word he coined in 1914, was a household topic among American modernist poets. In his "Vorticism" essay, in which his haiku-like poem, "The apparition of these faces in the crowd: / Petals, on a wet, black bough," was published, Pound theorized a poetic image not as a decorative emblem or symbol but as a seed capable of germinating and developing into another organism.[5] He presented this haiku-like poem as an illustration of his theory. Pound's insistence that an image in poetry must be active rather than passive suggests that a poem is not a description of something, but, as Aristotle said of tragedy, an action. Pound approaches Aristotelianism in his insistence that the image of the faces in the crowd in his Metro poem was not simply a description of his sensation at the station, but an active entity capable of dynamic development. In his experience, this particular image instantly transformed itself into another image, that of the petals on a wet, black bough.

    While Kerouac was not interested in such an influential modernist poet like Pound, he was enormously interested in the works of scholars on Japanese poetics and haiku in particular. As *The Dharma Bums* shows, Kerouac, while writing haiku, consulted Blyth's four-volume *Haiku*, noted earlier, as well as the complete works of D. T. Suzuki, a Japanese-British scholar of Zen and a friend and teacher of Blyth. Kerouac, however, never met Blyth or Suzuki in person, but he met in Berkeley, California, Arthur Waley, another foremost scholar of Japanese poetics.[6]

Waley has been well known over the generations by students and scholars of Japanese poetics for his work, *The Nō Plays of Japan*, first published in 1920. Pound and Yeats both consulted this book; it influenced their approaches to and understandings of noh play and Japanese poetics. Waley in this work and other studies demonstrated the philosophic and aesthetic principles that underlie Japanese poetics. For the creation of images in haiku, Kerouac was always interested in how classic haiku poets constructed images based on the aesthetic principles.

Blyth demonstrated with many classic haiku quoted that the aesthetic principle called "yugen" is based on Zen philosophy. Philosophically, an image of *yugen* depicts an object in nature devoid of human subjectivity. Aesthetically, such an image is often nebulous and hard for human eye to see. Originally *yugen* in Japanese art was an element of style pervasive in the language of *noh*. In reference to the *Works* by Zeami, the author of many of the extant *noh* plays, Waley expounds this difficult term *yugen*:

> It is applied to the natural grace of a boy's movements, to the gentle restraint of a nobleman's speech and bearing. "When notes fall sweetly and flutter delicately to the ear," that is the *yūgen* of music. The symbol of *yūgen* is "a white bird with a flower in its beak." "To watch the sun sink behind a flower-clad hill, to wander on and on in a huge forest with no thought of return, to stand upon the shore and gaze after a boat that goes hid by far-off islands, to ponder on the journey of wild-geese seen and lost among the clouds"—such are the gates to *yūgen*.[7]

The scenes Waley describes convey a feeling of satisfaction and release as does the catharsis of a Greek play, but *yugen* differs from catharsis because it has little to do with the emotional stress caused by tragedy. *Yugen* functions in art as a means by which human beings can comprehend the course of nature. The style of *yugen* can express either happiness or sorrow. Cherry blossoms, however beautiful they may be, must fade away; love between man and woman is inevitably followed by sorrow.

This mystery and inexplicability, which surrounds the order of the universe, had a strong appeal to a classic haiku poet like Basho, whose oft-quoted "The Old Pond" is exemplary:

> The old pond:
> A frog jumps in,—
> The sound of the water.

> (Translation by Blyth)[8]

This haiku shows that while the poet describes a natural phenomenon real-istically, he conveys his instant perception that nature is infinitely deep and absolutely silent. Such attributes of nature are not ostensibly stated; they are hidden. The tranquillity of the old pond with which the poet was struck remained in the background. He did not write "The rest is quiet"; instead he wrote the third line of the verse to read: "The sound of the water." The con-cluding image was given as a contrast to the background enveloped in silence. Basho's mode of expression is suggestive rather than descriptive, hidden and reserved rather than overt and demonstrative. *Yugen* has all the connotations of modesty, concealment, depth, and darkness. In Zen painting, woods and bays, as well as houses and boats, are hidden; hence these objects suggest infinity and profundity. Detail and refinement, which would mean limitation and temporariness of life, destroy the sense of permanence and eternity.

Kerouac tried to depict a scene in nature with *yugen* in such haiku as the following:

Content, the top trees
    shrouded
In gray fog

                    (*Book of Haikus* 85)

Everywhere beyond
    the Truth,
Empty space blue

                    (*Book of Haikus* 86)

I called Hanshan
    in the fog—
Silence, it said

                    (*Book of Haikus* 93)

The first and third haiku, "Content, the Top Trees" and "I called Hanshan," are both focused on an image of fog. In each haiku the fog hides whatever the poet is looking for. In "I called Hanshan" the poet is seeking an answer from Hanshan, a Medieval Chinese Zen poet known for his famous poem "Cold Mountain."[9] Hanshan's answer is silence, which is mysterious. The image of silence is also analogous to the Zen concept of *mu*. The second haiku, "Everywhere Beyond," also thrives not only on an image of *yugen*, "Empty space blue," that is mysterious, but also on the Zen state of mind, emptying of one's mind.

Many of Kerouac's haiku reflect his interest in Zen philosophy, the philosophy that underlies much of classic haiku, such as Basho's "The Old Pond." A Zen-inspired poet suppresses human subjectivity as much as possible, or minimize it, in depicting an object in nature, as well as an event in human life. Many of Kerouac's haiku that depict nonhumans, such as animals, birds, and insects, also reflect his interest in Buddhist ontology and the Buddhist theory of transmigration of the soul. In such haiku, Kerouac expresses profound respect and great compassion for nonhumans as does classic haiku poet like Issa. Grown up a Christian, Kerouac in his haiku conflated the Buddhist doctrine of compassion with the Cristian doctrine of mercy. Like Thoreau, he was inspired by Christianity as well as by Buddhism.

All in all, classic haiku taught Kerouac that not only must human beings treat their fellow human beings with respect and compassion, but they must also treat nonhuman beings as their equals. Classic haiku showed him the worldview that human beings are not at the center of the universe.

NOTES

1. In *A Week on the Concord and Merrimack Rivers* (1849), Thoreau wrote, "We can tolerate all philosophies, Atomists, Pneumatologists, Atheists, Theoists,—Plato, Aristotle, Leucippus, Democritus, Pythagoras, Zoroaster and Confucius. It is the attitude of these men, more than any communication which they make, that attracts us" (152). In the conclusion of "Civil Disobedience," Thoreau evoked Confucius: "The progress from an absolute to a limited monarchy, from a limited monarchy to a democracy, is a progress toward a true respect for the individual. Even the Chinese philosopher was wise enough to regard the individual as the basis of the empire" (*Variorum Civil Disobedience* 55).

2. John Tytell observes, "Kerouac . . . attacked the concept of revision sacred to most writers as a kind of secondary moral censorship imposed by the unconscious" (Naked Angels 17).

3. The translation is by Hakutani.

4. Masaoka Shiki (1867–1902), a modernist haiku poet, challenged the tradition of haiku established by Basho in the seventeenth century and Buson and Issa in the eighteenth century by writing his controversial essay "Criticism of Basho."

5. See Ezra Pound, "Vorticism," *Fortnighly Review*, n. s., no. 573 (September 1, 1914), 461–71.

6. In the *Dharma Bums*, Kerouac describes his meeting with Arthur Waley at a party he gave in Berkeley, California:

Nobody seemed to mind. In fact I saw Cacoethes and Arthur Whane [Waley] well-dressed standing having a polite conversation in the firelight with the two naked madmen, a kind of serious conversation about world affair. Finally Japhy

[Snyder] also got naked and wandered around with his jug. Every time one of his girls looked at him he gave a loud roar and leaped at them and they ran out of the house squealing. It was insane. I wondered what would ever happen if the cops in Corte Madera got wind of this and came roarin up the hill in their squad cars. The bonfire was bright, anybody down the road could see everything that was going on in the yard. Nevertheless it was strangely not out of place to see the bonfire, the food on the board, hear the guitar players, see the dense trees swaying in the breeze and a few naked men in the party. (196)

7. Waley further shows with Zeami's works that the aesthetic principle of yugen originated from Zen Buddhism. "It is obvious," Waley writes, "that Seami [Zeami] was deeply imbued with the teachings of Zen, in which cult Yoshimitsu may have been his master." See Author Waley, *Nō Plays of Japan* (New York: Grove, 1920), 21–22.

8. See R. H. Blyth, *Haiku: Eastern Culture* (Tokyo: Hokuseido Press, 1981), 302.

9. In the *Dharma Bums*, Kerouac and Snyder have a discussion of Han Shan's "Cold Mountain," which Snyder translated. One late cold afternoon Kerouac found Snyder sitting in the little shack in Berkeley "with his spectacles on, making him look old and scholarly and wise, with book on lap and the little tin teapot and porcelain cup steaming at his side." Kerouac said, "What you doing?" Snyder responded, "Translating Han Shan's great poem called 'Cold Mountain' written a thousand years ago some of it scribbled on the sides of cliffs hundreds of miles away from any other living beings" (19). The following is the opening lines of Snyder's translation:

Cold Mountain is a house
Without beams or walls.
The six doors left and right are open
The hall is blue sky.
The rooms all vacant and vague
The east wall beats on the wall
At the center nothing.

(McMichael, *Anthology of American Literature II* 1758).

Not only does this poem thrive on an image of open space that is mysterious, it also expresses the Zen concept of mu, "At the center nothing."

Part I

HISTORY AND CRITICISM

Chapter 1

The Genesis and Development of Haiku in Japan

Like transcendentalists such as Emerson and Whitman, Japanese haiku poets were inspired by nature, especially its beautiful scenes and seasonal changes. Japanese haiku had an affinity with transcendentalist poetry in light of the poet's attitude toward nature. Classic haiku poets and transcendentalist poets both viewed nature as a representation of divinity as well as of humanity. Although the exact origin of haiku is not clear, the close relationship haiku has with nature suggests the ways in which the ancient Japanese people lived on those islands. Where they came from is unknown but they must have adapted their living to ways of nature. Many were farmers, others hunters, fishermen, and warriors. While they often confronted nature, they always tried to live in harmony with it: Buddhism and Shintoism[1] constantly taught them that the soul existed in them as well as in nature, the animate and the inanimate alike, and that nature must be preserved as much as possible. Haiku traditionally avoided such subjects as earthquakes, floods, illnesses, and eroticism—ugly aspects of nature. Instead haiku poets were drawn to such objects as flowers, trees, birds, sunset, the moon, and genuine love. While those who earned their livelihood by labor had to battle with the negative aspects of nature, noblemen, priests, writers, singers, and artists found beauty and pleasure in natural phenomena. Since the latter group of people had the time to idealize or romanticize nature and impose a philosophy on it, they became an elite group of Japanese culture. Basho was an essayist, Buson a painter, and Issa a Buddhist priest, and also each being an accomplished haiku poet.

The genesis of haiku can be seen in the *waka* (Japanese song), the oldest verse form of thirty-one syllables in five lines (5–7–5–7–7), mentioned in the introduction. The first three lines of the *waka* are arranged 5–7–5, with such exceptions as 5–7–6 and 5–8–5. *One Hundred Poems by One Hundred Poets* (*Hyakunin Isshu*), a *waka* anthology compiled by Fujiwara no Sadaiye

(1162–1241) in 1235 contains haiku-like verses. Sadaiye's "The Falling Blossoms" ("Chiru Hana wo"), for example, reads,

The falling blossoms:
Look at them, it is the storm
That is chasing them.[2]

[*Chiru hana wo*
Oikakete yuku
Arashi kana]

(Henderson 10)

The focus of this verse is the poet's observation of a natural object, the falling blossoms. To a beautiful picture Sadaiye adds his feeling about this phenomenon: it looks as though a storm is pursuing the falling flower petals.

This seventeen-syllable verse form had been preserved by noblemen, courtiers, and high-ranked samurai for over two centuries since the publication of *One Hundred Poems by One Hundred Poets*. As noted in the introduction, around the beginning of the sixteenth century the verse form became popular among the poets. It was a dominant element of another popular verse form, *renga* (linked song), a continuous chain of fourteen (7–7) and seventeen (5–7–5) syllable verses, each independently composed, but connected as one poem. The first collection of *renga*, *Chikuba Singers' Collection* (*Chikuba Kyogin Shu*), 1499, contains over two hundred *tsukeku* (adding verses) linked with the first verses of another poet. As the word *kyogin* in the title of this collection implies, linked verses are generally characterized by a display of ingenuity and coarse humor. *Chikuba Singers' Collection* also collected twenty *hokku* (starting verses). Because the *hokku* was considered the most important verse of a *renga* series, it was usually composed by the senior poet attending *a renga* session. The fact that this collection included a much fewer number of *hokku* in proportion to *tsukeku* indicates the poets' interest in the comic nature of the *renga*.[3]

By the time Basho wrote that famous poem on the frog jumping into the old pond, *haikai*, an older poetic genre from which haiku evolved, had become a unique expression of poetic vision. Basho's poem was totally different from most of the *haikai* poems written by his predecessors: it was the creation of a new perception and not merely an ingenious play on words. As most scholars observe, the changes and innovations brought about in *haikai* poetry were not accomplished by a single poet. Basho's contemporaries, with Basho as their leader, attempted to create the serious *haikai*, a verse form known in modern times as haiku.[4] The haiku, then, was a highly uncommon genre that was short but could give more than wit or humor: a haiku late in the seventeenth century became a crystallized expression of one's vision and sensibility.

Because of their brevity and condensation, haiku seldom provide the picture with detail. The haiku poet delineates only an outline or highly selective parts and the reader must complete the vision. Above all, a classic haiku, as opposed to a modern one, is required to include a clear reference to one of the four seasons, as noted earlier. In Basho's "The Old Pond," said to be written in the spring of 1686, a seasonal reference to spring is made by the frog in the second line: the plunging of a single frog into the deep water suddenly breaks the deadly quiet background. Although the frog is traditionally a *kigo*, (seasonal word) of spring, some critics have considered this haiku evokes a scene in autumn, because it draws at once a picture of an autumnal desolation reigning over an ancient temple pond. As a result, the poet's perception of the infinitely quiet universe is intensified. It is also imperative that a haiku be primarily concerned with nature; if a haiku deals with human life, that life must be viewed in the context of nature rather than society.

The predilection to portray human life in association with nature means that the poet is more interested in genuinely human sentiments than in moral, ethical, or political problems. The following haiku by Kaga no Chiyo (1703–75), a famous woman poet in her age, illustrates that haiku thrives on the affinity between humanity and nature:

A morning glory
Has taken the well bucket:
I'll borrow water.

[*Asagao ni*
Tsurube torarete
0Morai mizu[5]]

Since a fresh, beautiful morning glory has grown on her well bucket over-night, Chiyo does not mind going over to her neighbor's to borrow water. Not only does her action show a desire to preserve nature, but the poem also expresses a natural and tender feeling one has for nature. A classic haiku, while it shuns human-centered emotions, thrives on such a nature-centered feeling as Chiyo's. This sensibility cannot be explained by logic or reason. Longer poems are often filled with intellectualized or moralized reasoning, but haiku avoids such language.

Because haiku is limited in its length, it must achieve its effect by a sense of unity and harmony within. Feelings of unity and harmony, reflective of Zen philosophy, as well as of Confucianism, are motivated by a desire to perceive every instant in nature and life: an intuition that nothing is alone, nothing is out of the ordinary. The unity of sentiment in haiku, as noted in the introduction, is intensified by the poet's expression of the senses. The

transference of the senses may occur between color and mood, as shown in a
haiku by Usuda Aro, a contemporary Japanese poet:

Were my wife alive,
I thought, saw a morning glory:
It has blossomed red.

[*Tsuma araba*
Tozo mou asagao
Akaki saku[6]]

The first line conveys a feeling of loneliness, but the red morning glory
reminds him of a happy life they spent together when she was living. The
redness, rather than the whiteness or blue color of the flower, is transferred
to the feeling of happiness and love. The transference of the senses, in turn,
gives the expression a sense of balance and harmony. His recollection of
their happy marriage, a feeling evoked by the red flower, compensates for the
death of his wife, a reality.

Well-wrought haiku thrive on the fusion of humanity and nature, and
on the intensity of love and beauty it creates. A haiku by Takarai Kikaku
(1661–1707), Basho's first disciple and one of the more innovative poets, as
noted in the introduction, is exemplary:

The harvest moon:
Lo, on the tatami mats
The Shape of a pine.

[*Meigetsu ya*
Tatami-no ue ni
Matsu-no-kage[7]]

The beauty of the moonlight depicted in this haiku is not only humanized,
since the light is shining on the human-made object, but also intensified by
the shadows of a pine tree falling on the mats. The beauty of the shadow
reflected on the human-made object is far more luminous than the light itself,
for the intricate pattern of an ageless pine tree as it stamps the dustless mats
intensifies the beauty of the moonlight. Not only does such a scene unify the
image of humanity and that of nature, but humanity and nature also interact.

As haiku has developed over the centuries, it has established certain aesthetic principles. To define and illustrate them is difficult since they refer
to subtle perceptions and complex states of mind in the creation of poetry.
Above all, these principles are governed by the national character developed
over the centuries. Having changed in meaning, they do not necessarily mean

the same today as they did in the seventeenth century. Discussion of these terms, furthermore, proves difficult simply because poetic theory does not always correspond to what poets actually write. It has also been true that the aesthetic principles for haiku are often applied to other genres of Japanese art such as *noh* play, flower arrangement, and the tea ceremony.

One of the most delicate principles of Eastern art is *yugen*. Originally *yugen* in Japanese art was an element of style pervasive in the language of *noh*. *Yugen* functions in art as a means by which human beings can comprehend the course of nature. Although *yugen* seems allied with a sense of resignation, it has a far different effect on the human psyche. A certain type of *noh* play like *Takasago* celebrates the order of the universe ruled by heaven. The mode of perception in the play may be compared to that of a pine tree with its evergreen needles, the predominant representation on the stage. The style of *yugen* can express either happiness or sorrow. Cherry blossoms, however beautiful they may be, must fade away; love between man and woman is inevitably followed by sorrow. *Yugen* has all the connotations of modesty, concealment, depth, and darkness. In Zen painting, woods and bays, as well as houses and boats, are hidden; hence, these objects suggest infinity and profundity. Detail and refinement, which would mean limitation and temporariness of life, destroy the sense of permanence and eternity.

Sabi, another frequently used term in Japanese poetics, implies that what is described is aged. Buddha's portrait hung in Zen temples, as the Chinese painter Lian K'ai's *Buddha Leaving the Mountains* suggests, exhibits the Buddha as an old man in contrast to the young figure typically shown in other temples.[8] Zen's Buddha looks emaciated, his environment barren; his body, his tattered clothes, the aged tree standing nearby, the pieces of dry wood strewn around, all indicate that they have passed the prime of their life and function. In this kind of portrait the old man with the thin body is nearer to his soul as the old tree with its skin and leaves fallen is to the very origin and essence of nature.

Sabi is traditionally associated with loneliness. Aesthetically, however, this mode of sensibility is characteristic of grace rather than splendor; it suggests quiet beauty as opposed to robust beauty. Basho's oft-quoted "A Crow," best illustrates this principle:

> A crow
> Perched on a withered tree
> 　　In the autumn evening.

(Blyth, History 2: xxix)

Loneliness suggested by a single crow on a branch of an old tree is reinforced by the elements of time indicated by nightfall and autumn. The picture is drawn with little detail and the overall mood is created by a simple, graceful description of fact. Furthermore, parts of the picture are delineated, by implication, in dark colors: the crow is black, the branch dark brown, the background dusky. The kind of beauty associated with the loneliness in Basho's poem is in marked contrast to the robust beauty depicted in a haiku by Mukai Kyorai (1651–1704), one of Basho's disciples:

> The guardians
> Of the cherry blossoms
>   Lay their white heads together.

> [*Hanamori ya*
> *Shiroki kashira wo*
>   *Tsuki awase*]

(Blyth, *History* 2: vii)

The tradition of haiku established in the seventeenth century produced eminent poets such as Buson and Issa in the eighteenth century, but the revolt against this tradition took place toward the end of the nineteenth century under the banner of a young poet, Masaoka Shiki (1867–1902). On the one hand, Basho's followers, except for Kikaku, instead of becoming innovators as was their master, resorted to an artificiality reminiscent of the comic *renga*. On the other hand, Issa, when he died, left no disciples. The Meiji restoration (1868) called for changes in all aspects of Japanese culture and Shiki became a leader in the literary revolution. He launched an attack on the tradition by publishing his controversial essay "Criticism of Basho." In response to a haiku by Hattori Ransetsu (1654–1707), Basho's disciple, Shiki composed his own. Ransetsu's haiku had been written two centuries earlier:

Yellow and white chrysanthemums:
What other possible names?
None can be thought of.

[*Ki-giku shira-giku*
Sono hoka-no na wa
Naku-mogana]

To Ransetsu's poem, Shiki responded with this one:

Yellow and white chrysanthemums:
But at least another one—
I want a red one.

[*Kigiku shira-giku*
Hito moto wa aka mo
Aramahoshi[9]]

Shiki advised his followers that they compose haiku to please themselves. To Shiki, some of the conventional haiku lack direct, spontaneous expressions: a traditional haiku poet in his or her adherence to old rules of grammar and devices such as *kireji* (cutting word), resorted to artificially twisting words and phrases.

A modernist challenge that Shiki gave the art of haiku, however, was to keep intact such aesthetic principles as *yugen* and *sabi*. Classic poets like Basho and Issa, who adhered to such principles, were also devout Buddhists. By contrast, Shiki, while abiding by the aesthetic principles, was considered an agnostic: his philosophy of life is shown in this haiku:

The wind in autumn
As for me there are no gods,
There are no Buddhas.

[*Aki-kaze ya*
Ware-ni kami nashi
Hokoke nashi[10]]

Although his direct reference to the divinities of Japanese culture smacks of a modernist style, the predominant image created by "the wind in autumn," a conventional *kigo* (seasonal word), suggests a deep-seated sense of loneliness and coldness. Shiki's mode of expression in this haiku is based on *sabi*.

Some well-known haiku poets in the twentieth century also preserve the sensibility of *sabi*. The predicament of a patient described in this haiku by Ishida Hakyo (1913–69) arouses *sabi*:

In the hospital room
I have built a nest box but
Swallows appear not.

[*Byo shitsu ni*
Subako tsukuredo
Tsubame kozu[11]]

Not only do the first and third lines express facts of loneliness, but also the patient's will to live suggested by the second line evokes a poignant sensibility. To a modernist poet like Hakyo, the twin problems of humanity are loneliness and boredom. He sees the same problems exist in nature as this haiku by him shows:

> The caged eagle;
When lonely
> He flaps his wings.

> [*Ori no washi*
Sabishiku nareba
> *Hautsu ka mo*]

(Blyth, *History* 2: 347)

The feeling of *sabi* is also evoked by the private world of the poet, the situation others cannot envision as this haiku by Nakamura Kusatao (1901–83), another modernist, shows:

At the faint voices
Of the flying mosquitoes
I felt my remorse.

[*Ka no koe no*
Hisoka naru toki
Kui ni keri[12]]

Closely related to *sabi* is a poetic sensibility called "*wabi*." Traditionally *wabi* has been defined in sharp antithesis to a folk or plebeian saying, "*Hana yori dango*" (Rice dumplings are preferred to flowers). Some poets are inspired by the sentiment that human beings desire beauty more than food, what is lacking in animals and other nonhuman beings. *Wabi* refers to the uniquely human perception of beauty stemmed from poverty. *Wabi* is often considered religious as the saying "Blessed are the poor" implies, but the spiritual aspect of *wabi* is based on the aesthetic rather than the moral sensibility.

Rikyu, the famed artist of the tea ceremony, wrote that food that is enough to sustain the body and a roof that does not leak are sufficient for human life. For Basho, however, an empty stomach was necessary to create poetry. Among Basho's disciples, Rotsu (1649–1738), the beggar-poet, is well known for having come into Basho's legacy of *wabi*. This haiku by Rotsu best demonstrates his state of mind:

> The water-birds too
Are asleep
> On the lake of Yogo?

[*Toridomo mo*
Neitte iru ka
　　Yogo no umi]

(Blyth, *History* 2: viii–ix)

Rotsu portrays a scene with no sight or sound of birds on the desolate lake. The withered reeds rustle from time to time in the chilly wind. It is only Rotsu the beggar and artist who is awake and is able to capture the beauty of the lake.

The sensibilities of *yugen*, *sabi*, and *wabi* all derive from the ways in which Japanese poets have seen nature over the centuries. Although the philosophy of Zen, on which the aesthetics of a poet like Basho is based, shuns emotion and intellect altogether, haiku in its modernist development by such a poet as Shiki, is often concerned with one's feeling and thought. If haiku expresses the poet's feeling, human subjectivity, that feeling must be generated by nature.

NOTES

1. Shintoism had been the national religion since as early as the fifth century until the end of World War II. Unlike other religions, it has neither scriptures nor doctrines. Traditionally, Shintoism teaches the followers to worship gods of natural forces and the Emperor as a descendant of the sun-goddess called *Ama-Terasu Ohmi Kami* (Heaven-Shining Great God) that rules the universe. Ever since Buddhism was introduced to Japan in the sixth century, Shintoism and Buddhism have coexisted in Japanese culture. As a result, a great majority of the Japanese people are Buddhists as well as Shintoists. Although haiku has more to do with Buddhism than Shintoism, the relation of Shintoism to haiku is a vital one, for haiku and Shintoism both express devotion to and veneration of nature.

2. The translation of this verse and other Japanese poems quoted in this book, unless otherwise noted, are by Hakutani.

3. Donald Keene notes, "The humor in *Chikuba Kyōgin Shū* has been characterized as 'tepid.' The same might be said of the *haikai* poetry composed by Arakida Moritake (1473–1549), a Shinto priest from the Great Shrine at Ise who turned from serious to comic renga late in life, and has been customarily styled (together with Sōkan) as a founder of haikai no renga" (Keene 13–14).

4. A detailed historical account of *haikai* poetry is given in Keene 337–57.

5. The original of "A Morning-Glory" is quoted from Fujio Akimoto, *Haiku Nyumon* (Tokyo: Kodansha, 1971), 23.

6. The original of "Were My Wife Alive" is quoted from Akimoto 200.

7. The original of "The Harvest Moon" is quoted from Henderson 58.

8. See Max Loehr, *The Great Paintings of China* (New York: Harper and Row, 1980), 216.

9. The originals of both haiku are quoted from Henderson 160.

10. The original is quoted from Henderson 164.

11. The original is quoted from Akimoto 222.

12. The original is quoted from Blyth, *History,* 2 vol. (Tokyo: Hokuseido, 1963), 322.

Chapter 2

Basho and Classic Haiku Tradition

The tradition of classic haiku was established by Matsuo Basho (1644–1694). By 1680, when Basho composed the first version of his celebrated haiku on a frog jumping in the water, haiku had become a highly styled expression of poetic vision:

The old pond:
A frog jumped in —
The sound of the water.

(translation by Hakutani)

[Furu ike ya
Kawazu tobi komu
Mizu no oto]

Basho's haiku such as "The Old Pond," unlike those of his predecessors, represented a new perspective in depicting nature and did not rely on an ingenious play on words often seen in *renga* (linked verse), a poetic genre popular among his predecessors. Basho attempted to compose the serious haiku, a unique poetic genre that was short but was able to express more than wit or humor. Because of its brevity and condensation, a haiku seldom provides details. The haiku poet draws only an outline or a highly selective image, and the reader must complete the vision. Above all, a classic haiku, as opposed to a modernist one, is required to include *kigo* (seasonal word) in reference to one of the four seasons.

To explain Basho's art of haiku, Yone Noguchi, a noted bilingual poet and critic, once quoted "The Old Pond," perhaps the most frequently quoted haiku in haiku criticism: "The old pond! / A frog leapt into— / List, the water sound!"[1] One may think a frog is an absurd poetic subject, but Basho focused his vision on a scene of desolation, an image of nature. The pond was perhaps situated on the premises of an ancient temple whose silence was suddenly broken by a frog plunging into the deep water. As Noguchi conceived the experience, Basho, a Zen Buddhist, was "supposed to awaken into enlightenment now when he heard the voice bursting out of voicelessness, and the conception that life and death were mere change of condition was deepened into faith" (*Selected English Writings* 2: 74). Basho was not suggesting that the tranquillity of the pond meant death or that the frog symbolized life. Basho here had the sensation of hearing the sound bursting out of soundlessness. A haiku is not a representation of goodness, truth, or beauty; there is nothing particularly good, true, or beautiful about a frog leaping into the water.

It seems as though Basho, in writing the poem, carried nature within him and brought himself to the deepest level of nature, where all sounds lapse into the world of silence and infinity. Though his vision is based on reality, it transcends time and space. What a Zen poet like Basho is showing is that one can do enough naturally, enjoy doing it, and achieve one's peace of mind. This fusion of humanity and nature is called spontaneity in Zen. The best haiku, because of their linguistic limitations, are inwardly extensive and outwardly infinite. A severe constraint imposed on one aspect of haiku must be balanced by a spontaneous, boundless freedom on the other.

Basho's haiku is not only an expression of sensation, but it is also a generalization and depersonalization of that sensation. This characteristic can be shown by one of Basho's lesser-known haiku:

How cool it is!
Putting the feet on the wall:
An afternoon nap.

[Hiya-hiya to
Kabe wo fumaete
Hiru-ne kana[2]]

Basho was interested in expressing how his feet, anyone's feet, would feel when placed on a cool wall in the house on a warm summer afternoon. His sensation suggests that any other person would also enjoy the experience. Basho did not want to convey any emotion, any thought, any beauty; there remained only poetry, only nature.

That the art of haiku comes from human beings' affinity with nature is best explained by Basho in his travelogue *Manuscript in My Knapsack* (*Oi no Kobumi*):

One and the same thing runs through the waka of Saigyō, the renga of Sōgi, the paintings of Sesshū, the tea ceremony of Rikyū. What is common to all these arts is their following nature and making a friend of the four seasons. Nothing the artist sees but is flowers, nothing he thinks of but is the moon. When what a man sees is not flowers, he is no better than a barbarian. When what he thinks in his heart is not the moon, he belongs to the same species as the birds and beasts. I say, free yourselves from the barbarian, remove yourself from the birds and beasts; follow nature and return to nature.[3]

Basho's admonition in the passage suggests that haiku is the creation of things that already exist in nature but requires the artistic sensibility of a poet. What Basho is seeking in haiku composition is not beauty as in *waka*, but significance that underlies such an image as a jumping frog, a barking dog, a chirping cicada, or a bird on a branch.

To elicit significance from an image, the haiku poet must verify its existence. The image is concrete: Basho always emphasizes the material, as against the so-called spiritual. For him, there is no abstract arguing, no general principles. His haiku is focused on the expression of a temporary enlightenment, in which the reader sees into life of things. Although critics often relate Basho's enlightenment to Zen philosophy, it is not a matter of life and death for the soul. It is focused on life and its moment, however temporary it may be. As "On a Withered Branch" ("On a withered branch / A lone crow has been perching / Autumn evening"[4]) shows, that moment of revelation is clinched by the larger context suggested by "Autumn evening," a seasonal reference. It is toward the end of a year and at the end of a day. A crow, a lone figure, is resting on a withered branch. All these images are affecting the feeling of the poet. Not only does Basho's haiku exhibit a poignant interaction between the subjective and the objective, but there also emerges a unity of feeling that permeates the poem.

As his prose works, such as *Manuscript in My Knapsack* (*Oi no Kobumi*) and *Narrow Road to the Interior* (*Oku no Hosomichi*), suggest, Basho created his haiku out of his own imagination and experience. But critics have pointed out his worldview was influenced by ancient philosophies and religions such as Confucianism, Buddhism, and Zen. "Confucianism," R. H. Blyth notes, "contributed a certain sobriety, reserve, lack of extravagance and hyperbole, brevity and pithiness, and a moral flavour that may sometimes be vaguely felt, but is never allowed to be separated, as it is in Wordsworth and Hakura-kuten, from the poetry itself" (*Haiku* 71).[5]

Basho was well versed in *The Analects*, which consists of maxims and parables that illustrate Confucian ethics. Confucian ethics, as noted in the introduction, may be defined as a code of honor by which the individual must live in society. It consists of four virtues written in Chinese characters: 仁 (Humanity), 義 (Justice), 忠 (Loyalty), and 孝 (Filial Piety). Basho, who read

The Analects, wrote many haiku that express Confucian virtues. Basho wrote, for example, such a haiku as:

> The dew of the camphor tree
> Falls in tears
>   On the pinks.

> [Nadeshiko ni
> Kararu namida ya
>   Kusunoki no trsuyu]

>   (*Haiku* 82)

Basho drew an analogy between the virtue of loyalty and the dew of the camphor tree. This haiku, R. H. Blyth notes, "refers to Kusunoki and his son Masatsura, when they parted, in 1336, before the father's defeat and suicide" (*Haiku* 82).

As "The Dew of the Camphor Tree," suggests that, for Basho, Confucian virtues are derived from human sentiments as well as from natural phenomena. "This simple Confucianism," Blyth observes, "developed into something deeper and wider, embracing all nature in its scope, without losing its human feeling" (*Haiku* 82–83). The following haiku also express Confucius's worldview:

> Nothing intimates
> How soon they must die,—
>   Crying cicadas.

> [*Yagate shinu*
> *Keshiki mo miezu*
>   *Semi no koe*]

> The morning
> After the gale too,
>   Peppers are red

> [*Ōkaze no*
> *Ashita mo Akashi*
>   *Tōgarashi*]

> The first snow,
> Just enough to bend
>   The leaves of the daffodils.

[*Hatsu-yuki ya
Suisen no ha no
   Tawamu made*]

(*Haiku* 83)

The Confucian worldview is also echoed by Nakae Toju (1608–1648), one of the greatest thinkers in Japanese history. Toju said, "Heaven and Earth and man appear to be different, but they are essentially one. This essence has no size, and the spirit of man and the infinite must be one" (*Haiku* 80).

The unity of humanity and nature is also stressed in the *Saikontan*, said to be written by Kojisei, a collection of 359 short passages and poems, which was widely known in the Ming Dynasty in China. One of the passages reads as follows:

> Water not disturbed by waves settles down of itself. A mirror not covered with dust is clear and bright. The mind should be like this. When what beclouds it passes away, its brightness appears. Happiness must not be sought for; when what disturbs passes away, happiness comes of itself. (*Haiku* 75)

Not only does this epigram demonstrate an affinity that exists between humanity and nature, it suggests that ethics is sanctioned by fact of nature rather than by human subjectivity. Another passage provides an illustration of the way in which the human mind learns from nature:

> The song of birds, the voices of insects, are all means of conveying truth to the mind; in flowers and grasses we see messages of the Way. The scholar, pure and clear of mind, serene and open of heart, should find in everything what nourishes him. (*Haiku* 76)

This maxim admonishes the reader against human subjectivity: the less subjective the mind is the more objective it becomes. The mind buttressed by nature thus enables ethics to be established.

In a later passage Kojisei states, "If your heart is without stormy waves, everywhere are blue mountains and green trees. If our real nature is creative like nature itself, wherever we may be, we see that all things are free like sporting fishes and circling kites" (*Haiku* 79). The human mind, as Kojisei observes, is often influenced by excessive emotion like anger. Once the mind is overwhelmed by such emotion and loses its control, it becomes alienated from ethics and universal truth. Kojisei's observation suggests that if human nature becomes destructive instead of creative like nature, it ceases to function.

Creation of ethics is possible, as Kojisei demonstrates, only if the mind is capable of seeing universal truth in nature, "The just man," Kojisei reasons, "has no mind to seek happiness; Heaven, therefore, because of this mind-lessness, opens its inmost heart." On the other hand, he sees, "the bad man busies himself with avoiding misfortunes; Heaven therefore confounds him for this desire." Contrasting nature with humanity, he says, "How unsearch-able are the ways of Heaven! How useless the wisdom of men!" (*Haiku* 75). What Kojisei calls "the ways of Heaven" are "unsearchable" and infinite; therefore, they constitute universal truth, the absolute values. Chapter XVI of *The Doctrine of the Mean*, a medieval Chinese text, quotes Confucius as follows: "Confucius said, 'The power of spirits, how abundant! We look, but do not see them; we listen, but do not hear them; yet they sustain all things, and nothing is neglected by them'" (*Haiku* 73).

In Confucius's work, the universe consists of 天 (Heaven), 地 (Earth), and 人 (Human). Some of the passages in *The Analects* express Confucius's thoughts and observations on the relationships among Heaven, Human, and God:

How can a man conceal his nature? How can a man
   conceal his nature? (*Analects* 2. 10).
He who offends against Heaven has none to whom he can pray (*Analects* 3. 12).
He sacrificed to the spirits [God] as if the spirits were present (*Analects* 3. 12).
A virtuous man finds rest in his virtue (*Analects* 4. 2).

(*Haiku* 73)

For Confucius, God is a concept that originates from the individual living in society. The individual thus formulates this concept by apprehending the ways of nature in Heaven and on Earth. God, therefore, reflects the con-science, a code of ethics established by the individual.

Confucianism is said to have inspired Japanese poets, including Basho. At the beginning of *The Analects* Confucius says, "Is it not delightful to have a friend come from afar?" This saying, Blyth notes, inspired Basho to compose this haiku:

   A paulownia leaf has fallen;
Will you not come to me
   In my loneliness?

   [*Sabishisa wo*
Toute kurenu ka
   Kiri hito-ha]

(*Haiku* 71)

The haiku was addressed to his fellow haiku poet Ransetsu. Basho's wish to share his poetic vision with others suggests that one can model one's life after a code of ethics best defined in poetic words. That Confucius's advice "Stand with propriety" is mediated between the two actions "Arise with poetry" and "Grow with music" defines the meaning of the word *propriety*. This word in Confucius means, as Blyth explains, "a harmonious mode of living . . . a poetical way of doing everything . . . a deep, inward rightness of relation between ourselves and all outward circumstances" (*Haiku* 72). Analects 9. 16 reads, "Standing by a stream, Confucius said, 'It ceases not day or night, flowing on and on like this'" (*Haiku* 72). Not only is Confucius's description of the scene poetic and beautiful to look at, it conveys universal truth.[6] In Confucius's work, an individual must establish himself or herself by adhering to universal ethics. Once these ethics become the foundation of the individual, no other ideas and facts are to undermine that foundation.

As Confucianism influenced Basho, so did Buddhism. He was a devout Buddhist all his life. Like Henry David Thoreau, an American transcendentalist who lived in close contact with nature, Basho traveled in the fields and the woods throughout his career. Both men were celibate; they were both fascinated with other living beings, animate or inanimate. That humans and nonhumans equally belong to the universe is a Confucian thought, and it is true of Buddhism. But, for Basho, there was a difference between Confucianism and Buddhism: Buddhism puts more emphasis on human compassion than does Confucianism. The doctrine that all things, even the inanimate, have the Buddha-nature distinguishes Buddhism from Confucianism. Whereas Confucianism defines a cosmology, Buddhism is concerned with human nature. The reason for Thoreau's attraction to Buddhism rather than to Christianity was his realization that Buddhists believed in the existence of the soul in animals as Christians did not.[7]

Basho's stronger interest in others than in himself is best shown by this well-known haiku:

> It is deep autumn:
> My neighbor—
> How does he live, I wonder?

> [*Aki fuka ki*
> *Tonari wa nani wo*
> *Suru hito zo*]

(*Haiku* 158)

Feelings of unity and comradery, reflective of the Buddhistic philosophy, are motivated by a desire to perceive every instant in nature and humanity, an intuition that nothing is alone, nothing is out of the ordinary. This haiku creates a sense of unity and relatedness in society. Though a serious poet, Basho was enormously interested in the commonplace and the common people. In this haiku, as autumn approaches winter and perhaps he nears the end of his life, he takes a deeper interest in his fellow human beings. His observations of the season and his neighbor, a total stranger, are separate, yet both observations intensify each other. His vision, as it is unified, evokes a deeply felt, natural, and universal sentiment—compassion.

Just as human beings are united with compassion, there is also no clear-cut distinction between human and nonhuman. "The polytheism of the ordinary Japanese, like that of the Greeks," Blyth observes, "had a great effect upon their mode of poetical life. The gods are many: Amaterasu, Miroku, Hachiman, Jizō, Amida, Dainichi Nyorai, Tenjin, Kwannon, Emma O, Shakamuni, Benten, and a hundred others. . . . But these gods are not far from us, either in place or in rank. . . . The scale of beings in the Buddhist universe puts man midway. The primitive animistic ideas of the Japanese fall in with the Buddhist system, and all are united by the theory of transmigration" *(Haiku* 19). The following haiku by Basho illustrates that the soul exists in human beings as well as in nonhuman beings:

> The god is absent;
> Dead leaves are piling,
>   An all is deserted.

> [*rusu no ma ni*
> *Aretaru kami no*
>   *Ochiba kana*]

(Haiku 19)

In this haiku our sympathies are widened in both directions, toward gods as well as toward dead leaves.

Some of Basho's haiku express his sympathy with nonhuman. His compassion on animals may have derived from the theory of transmigration, but the following haiku suggests that his sympathy with the animate sprang spontaneously from his experience:

> First winter rain:
> The monkey also seems
>   To want a small straw cloak.

> [*Hatsu-shigure*
> *Saru mo komino wo*
>   *Hosige nari*]

(Haiku 297)

"Basho," Blyth notes, "was once returning from Ise, the home of the gods, to his native place of sad memories. Passing through the lonely forest, the cold rain pattering on the fallen leaves, he saw a small monkey sitting huddled on a bough, with that submissive pathos which human beings can hardly attain to. Animals alone possess it" (*Haiku* 297). In a similar vein Basho expresses human sympathy with another living being:

> The octopuses in the jars
> Transient dreams
> Under the summer noon.

> [*Takotsuboya*
> *Hakanaki yume wo*
> *Natsu no tsuki*]

> (*Haiku* 22)

The doctrine that all living things possess the Buddha-nature accounts not only for a religious sentiment but also for an innate human sensibility.

Not only was Basho inspired by Buddhism, especially by its doctrine of mercy, he was deeply influenced by Zen philosophy. Many of his haiku depict that one can do enough naturally and freely, enjoy doing it, and achieve one's peace of mind. This fusion of humanity and nature is called spontaneity in Zen. From a Zen point of view, such a division is devoid of intellectualism and emotionalism. Since Zen is the most important philosophical tradition influencing Japanese haiku, as noted earlier, the haiku poet aims to understand the spirit of nature. Basho thus recognized little division between human and nature, man and woman, young and old; he was never concerned with the problems of good and evil.[8]

The most important concept that underlies Zen philosophy is the state of mind called *mu* or nothingness. In *A Travel Account of My Exposure in the Fields* (*Nozarashi Kiko*), one of Basho's earlier books of essays, he opens with this revealing passage with two haiku:

When I set out on my journey of a thousand leagues I packed no provisions for the road. I clung to the staff of that pilgrim of old who, it is said, "entered the realm of nothingness under the moon after midnight." The voice of the wind sounded cold somehow as I left my tumbledown hut on the river in the eighth moon of the Year of the Rat, 1684.

> Nozarashi wo   Bones exposed in a field—
> Kokoro ni kaze no   At the thought, how the wind
> Shimu mi ka na   Bites into my flesh.

Aki tō tose   Autumn—this makes ten years;
Kaette Edo wo   Now I really mean Edo
Sasu kokyō   When I speak of "home."

(Keene 81)

The first haiku conveys a sense of *wabi* because the image of his bones suggests poverty and eternity.[9] Although Basho endured fatigue and hardship on
his journey, he reached a higher state of mind.[10] While he was aware of his
physical and material poverty, his life was spiritually fulfilled. In this state of
mind, having nothing meant having all.

For Basho, to enter the state of nothingness, one must annihilate oneself.
The undisciplined self is often misguided by egotism. To live life freely, one
must suppress subjectivity. Doho, Basho's disciple, wrote the following:

> When the Master said, "As for the pine, learn from the pine; as for the bamboo,
> learn from the bamboo," he meant cast aside personal desire or intention. Those
> who interpret this "learning" in their own way end up never learning.
>
>   The phrase "learn" means to enter into the object, to be emotionally moved
> by the essence that emerges from that object, and for that movement to become
> verse. Even if one clearly expresses the object, if the emotion does not emerge
> from the object naturally, the object and the self will be divided, and that emo-
> tion will not achieve poetic truth [*makoto*]. The effect will be verbal artifice that
> results from personal desire. (Shirane 261)

Doho observed in Basho's haiku that the less subjective feeling is expressed
the more objective vision emerges. For example,

In the midst of the plain
        Sings the skylark,
Free of all things.

        [*Hara-naka ya*
Mono ni mo tsukazu
        Naku hibari]

        Sweeping the garden,
The snow is forgotten
        By the broom.

        [*niwa haite*
Yuki wo wasururu
        Hōki kana]

The mountains and garden also move;
The summer drawing room
Includes them.

[*Yama mo niwa mo
Ugoki iruru ya
Natsuzashiki*]

(*Haiku* 38)

The first haiku, "In the Midst of the Plain," depicts the state of nothingness: the skylark, singing freely, is not singing of himself. The second haiku, "Sweeping the Garden," represents the primacy of nature over humanity: the human activity is negated by a natural phenomenon. The third haiku, "The Mountains and Garden Also Move," exhibits the unity of nature and humanity: what appears to be a human creation turns out to be part of nature.

Another aspect of the state of nothingness is loneliness. Basho expresses human loneliness in such a haiku as this one:

Ah, *kankodori*,
Deepen thou
My loneliness.

[*Uki ware wo
Sabishi garaseyo
Kankodori*]

(*Haiku* 161–62)

While Basho portrays his loneliness, he intimates that he is not alone in nature. Even though the mountain bird's cry deepens his loneliness, it signifies that a living being is connected to another and that nothing is isolated in nature. Basho's expression of loneliness is reminiscent of Langston Hughes's expression of the blues sensibility. In "The Weary Blues," Hughes writes the following:

In a deep song voice with a melancholy tone
I heard that Negro sing, that old piano moan—
        "Ain't got nobody in all this world,
        Ain't got nobody but ma self.
        I's gwine to quit ma frownin'
        And put ma troubles on the shelf."

(*Selected Poems* 33)

Although the blues musician has no one with him, he keeps his soul intact with him. Like Basho, Hughes is portraying a state of isolation, loneliness, and poverty, which in turn enriches his soul.

The state of Zen, in which having nothing we possess all, implies paradox and contradiction. Rinzai (d. 867), a medieval Japanese Zen priest, was asked about the esoteric teaching of Daruma. He replied, "If there is any meaning in it, I myself am not saved." The interlocutor responded: "If it was meaningless, how was it the 2nd Patriarch (Eka) received the law?" Rinzai could only say, "This receiving is non-receiving" (*Haiku* 193). Basho's haiku "By Daylight," for instance, expresses such a paradox and contradiction:

> By daylight,
> The nape of the neck of the firefly
> Is red.
>
> [*Hiru mireba
> Kubisuji akaki
> Hotaru kana*]

(*Haiku* 200)

Basho was disillusioned, for in the dark the firefly emitted a golden light but by daylight it looked merely red. This haiku recalls Emily Dickinson's poem "Success Is Counted Sweetest":

> To comprehend a nectar
> Requires sorest need.

For Dickinson, success in life is best appreciated by failure. Only those who fail can cherish those who succeed:

> As he defeated—dying—
> On whose forbidden ear
> The distant strains of triumph
> Burst agonized and clear!

(*Complete Poems* 35)

Just as the state of Zen yields an expression of paradox and contradiction, so does her view of success.

A Zen point of view enables one to see things in humanity and nature more objectively. Zen teaches us to gain freedom from our ideas and desires. Basho composed a haiku such as the following:

To be rained upon, in winter,
And not even an umbrella-hat,—
Well, well!

[*Kasa mo naki
Ware wo shigururu
Nanto nanto*]

(*Haiku* 207)

From a human point of view, being rained on when you do not have an umbrella is uncomfortable. From nature's perspective, however, rain provides water for all objects in nature: water, nourishing plants and animals, creates more life on earth. Such a haiku has an affinity with Buson's haiku "An Autumn Eve":

An autumn eve;
There is joy too,
In loneliness.

[*Sabishisa no
Ureshiku mo ari
Aki no kure*]

(*Haiku* 208)

From a human point of view, one might feel lonely in autumn, but from nature's perspective, autumn is joyful. Basho's and Buson's haiku both suggest that human beings are not alienated from nature. Another haiku by Basho contrasts a human point of view with nature's perspective:

The Rose of Sharon
By the roadside,
Was eaten by the horse.

[*Michi-no-be- no
Mokuge wa uma ni
Kuware keri*]

(*Haiku* 217)

Basho was impressed with the beautiful rose of Sharon on the roadside, but the horse wanted to eat it. What he implies is something that belongs to Zen: our desires and subjectivity are not always in harmony with nature.

One of the salient techniques in Basho's haiku is a juxtaposition of images. In "The Old Pond," Basho made a stark contrast between the silence of the old pond and the sound of a jumping frog. In another famous haiku he also juxtaposed the silence that prevailed in the deep woods to the shrill voice of cicadas:

> How quiet it is!
> Penetrating the rocks
> > The cicada's voice.
>
> > > > > (Translation by Hakutani)

> [*Shizukesa ya*
> *Iwa ni shimiiru*
> > *Semi mo koe*]
>
> > > > > (*Haiku* 9)

Not only did Basho make a contrast between the opposing images, but he also juxtaposed the disparate ideas behind the images:

> bright harvest moon—
> on the viewing stand
> not one beautiful face

> [*meigetsu ya*
> *zani utsukushiki*
> *kao mo nashi*]
>
> > > > > (Shirane 103)

> The love of the cats;
> When it was over, the hazy moon
> > Over the bed-chamber.

> [*Neko no koi*
> *Yamu toki neya no*
> > *Oborozuki*]
>
> > > > > (*Haiku* 264)

In "Bright Harvest Moon," Basho depicted the beautiful harvest moon. As he turned his eyes away from the moon to the earth, he did not even see one beautiful face among the moon viewers. Expressing his disillusionment, he was also suggesting the supremacy of nature over humanity. In "The Loves of the Cats," he initially focused on the loud, intense love-making of the cats. This image was juxtaposed to the quiet image of the hazy moon over his bedroom. As the collision of thoughts or images stimulates the poet, his mind is encouraged to make the effort to overcome the difficulty of uniting nature and humanity.

Basho is also known for the use of *kireji* (cutting words) in juxtaposing the images. The classic *renga* (linked verse) had eighteen varieties of *kireji* for dividing its sections: *ya, kana, keri,* and so forth. Basho increased the variety to forty-eight as the use of *kireji* was refined and expanded. In "The Old Pond," mentioned earlier, *ya* is attached to the words *furu ike* (old pond): Basho is expressing a feeling of awe about the quietness of the pond. In "How Quiet It Is," Basho uses *ya* to emphasize the deadly quiet atmosphere of the woods he is visiting. Although "The Loves of the Cats" does not include a *kireji*, the first line is set off syntactically by the second line "*Yamu toki*" (When it was over). Above all, adding a *kireji* is a structural device to "cut" or divide a whole into parts. Since composing a haiku is confined to seventeen syllables in three line, the parts of a vision or idea must be clearly segmented and united in their development.

Another technique that characterizes Basho's haiku is the unity of sentiments created in portraying nature and humanity. In the following haiku he unites the subjective with the objective, humanity with nature:

a wild sea—
stretching out to Sado Isle
the Milky Way

[*araumi ya*
Sado ni yokotau
amanogawa]

(Shirane 263)

This haiku, describing a wild sea stretching out to Sado Island, a scene in nature Basho is watching, projects his own personal feeling. Relating the poet's emotive state to a scene in nature is reminiscent of T. S. Eliot's objective correlative. Eliot's "The Love Song of J. Alfred Prufrock" begins with these three lines:

Let us go then, you and I,
When the evening is spread out against the sky
Like a patient etherised upon a table;

(*Complete Poems* 3)

Eliot is projecting the feeling of a patient on an operating table in a hospital to the evening spreading out against the sky. In Basho's and Eliot's verses, the scene in nature is unified with the feeling of the individual.

Basho also creates unity in expressing the senses. In the following haiku, "Sinking into the Body" unifies the senses of color and temperature:

Sinking into the body
The bitterness of the daikon
The wind of autumn.

(Translation by Hakutani)

[*mi ni shimite*
daikon karashi
aki no kaze]

(Shirane 95)

The bitterness of the daikon, which depicts the senses of taste and color, is associated with the coldness of the autumn wind, a *kigo* (seasonal reference). The association of the senses is, in turn, related to the poet's feeling, the bitterness sinking into his body. In Basho's haiku, and indeed in classic haiku, the poet tries to relate human sentiments to nature. The use of *kigo* thus clarifies the poet's intention to unify the subjective with the objective, humanity and nature.

Seasonal reference in haiku functions as an objective correlative in relating the poet's sentiments to a phenomenon in nature. In associating the subjective with the objective, the poet focuses on an image in nature. The poet's aim is to depict the image that exists on its own object without reference to something other than itself.[11] As Ezra Pound observed, haiku is imagistic rather than symbolic. Whereas W. B. Yeats's symbolism was influenced by his cross-cultural visions of *noh* theatre and Irish folklore, Pound's imagism had its origin in classic haiku. In his essay "Vorticism," published in the *Fortnightly Review* in 1914, Pound defined the function of an image in haiku: an image is not a decorative emblem or symbol but a seed that germinates and develops into another organism. As an illustration, he composed what he called "a hokku-like sentence": "The apparition of these faces in the crowd: / Petals, on a wet, black bough" ("Vorticism" 467).

Pound's use of images in this poem has an affinity with Basho's in such a haiku as "On a Withered Branch" ("On a withered branch / A crow has just perched / Autumn evening"). As the image of the faces in the crowd and the image of the petals on a wet bough interact with each other in Pound's poem, so do the image of a crow on a withered branch and the image of autumn evening in Basho's haiku. Just as Pound actually saw these faces in the crowd, so did Basho see the crow momentarily resting on a branch. Each image made such a strong impression on the mind of the poet that the image transformed itself into another image. In Pound's poem, the outward, objective image of the faces in the crowd "darts into a thing inward and subjective," the image of the petals on a wet, black bough ("Vorticism" 467). Whereas the faces in the crowd were real, the petals on a bough were imaginary. Similarly, the outward, objective image of a crow on a withered branch transformed into the image of autumn evening in Basho's mind. Pound called the image of the petals on a wet, black bough inward and subjective, for it was newly created in his mind. Although this image appeared imaginary, describing the petals with a wet, black bough evoked an outward and objective scene in late autumn or winter. Likewise, the image of autumn evening in Basho's haiku was created in the mind but the description of the branch on which the crow perched as being withered made an inward, subjective image outward and objective.

Such a haiku as "On a Withered Branch" may be expressing the poet's feeling of loneliness, but this subjectivity is conveyed directly with a combination of objective images. The focus of Basho's vision is a lone crow. The branch the bird perches on is withered, the time is evening, and the season is autumn. These images, coalescing into a unified sensibility, suggest the emotive state of the poet. In Basho's haiku, nature exists as something real, concrete, and organic before his eyes, but at the same time nature, interacting with his mind, functions as a projection of his feelings. As a result, Basho's haiku is a simple, spontaneous expression of human sentiments. In the context of nature, Basho's expression of feelings becomes genuine, poignant, and free of any complicated or confused philosophical and social ideas.

NOTES

1. The translation of this haiku is by Noguchi, in *Selected English Writings of Yone Noguchi* 2: 73–74. Translations of other haiku quoted in this chapter are by R. H. Blyth unless otherwise noted.

2. The original is quoted from Henderson 49. The translation of this haiku, "How Cool It Is!" is by Hakutani.

3. Quoted and translated by Keene 93.

4. The translation of this haiku, "On a Withered Branch," is by Hakutani.

5. Haruo Shirane notes, "Bashō worked to assimilate the Chinese and Japanese poetic traditions into haikai and to appropriate the authority and aura of the ancients— whose importance grew in the late seventeenth century, as exemplified by the ancient studies of Confucian texts by Itō Jinsai (1627–1705) and the ancient studies of the *Man'yōshū* by Keichū (1640–1701). As we have seen, Bashō incorporated orthodox Neo-Confucian thought into haikai poetics, hoping to raise the status of haikai, give it a spiritual and cosmological backbone, and make it part of the larger poetic and cultural tradition" (289).

6. Confucias's description of this scene in the analects is remindful of John Keats's line "Beauty is truth, truth beauty" in "Ode on a Grecian Urn" (1819). Emily

Dickinson personifies beauty and truth in her poem "I Died for Beauty—but Was Scarce." Dickinson sees Beauty and Truth united in life and death:

He questioned softly, "Why I failed"?
"For Beauty", I replied—
"And I—for Truth—Themself are One—
We Brethren, are", He said—

And so, as Kinsmen, met a Night—
We talked between the Rooms—
Until the Moss had reached our lips—
And covered up—our names—
                    (*Complete Poems* 216)

7. As his first book, *A Week on the Concord and Merrimack Rivers* (1849), indicates Thoreau was fascinated with Buddhism. "It is necessary not to be Christian," Thoreau argued, "to appreciate the beauty and significance of the life of Christ. I know that some will have hard thoughts of me, when they hear their Christ named beside my Buddha, yet I am sure that I am willing they should love their Christ more than my Buddha" (*A Week* 67).

8. Walt Whitman, who was also influenced by Buddhism, wrote in "Song of Myself":

I am the poet of the Body and I am the poet of the Soul,
The pleasures of heaven are with me and the pains of hell are with me,
. . . .
I am the poet of the woman the same as the man,
                    (*Complete Poetry* 39)

These lines define the the the theme of "Song of Myself": like a Buddhist. Whitman does not distinguish between body and soul, good and evil, man and woman.

9. As noted earlier, *wabi* underlies the uniquely human perception of beauty derived from poverty. Referring to Basho's aesthetic principle, R. H. Blyth observes, "Without contact with the things, with cold and hunger, real poetry is impossible. Further, Bashō was a missionary spirit and knew that all over Japan were people capable of treading the Way of Haiku. But beyond this, just as with Christ, Bashō's heart was turned towards poverty and simplicity; it was his fate, his lot, his destiny as a poet" (*Haiku* 296).

10. According to R H. Blyth, Zen "means that state of mind in which we are not separated from other things, are indeed identical with them, and yet retain our own individuality and personal peculiarities . . . it means a body of experience and practice begun by Daruma, (who came to China 520 A. D.) as the practical application to living of Mahayana doctrines, and continued to the present day in Zen temples and Zen books of instruction" (*Haiku* 5).

11. While Blyth observes that an image in haiku does not function as a metaphor, Haruo Shirane argues that "haikai, like all poetry, is highly metaphorical: the essential difference, as we shall see, is that the metaphorical function is implicit rather than stated and often encoded in a polysemous phrase or word" (Shirane 46).

Chapter 3

Yone Noguchi and Modernist Haiku Poetics

Yone Noguchi was born in a small town near Nagoya in 1875. In the late 1880s the young Noguchi, taking great interest in English texts used in a public school, read Samuel Smiles's writings on self-help. Perhaps inspired by Smiles, but in any case dissatisfied with his public school instruction, he withdrew from a middle school in Nagoya and went to Tokyo in 1890. At a prep school there he diligently read such Victorian writings as Thomas Macauley's *Life of Samuel Johnson*, exactly the type of reading many a literary aspirant was doing on the other side of the Pacific.

A year later, detesting the national university an ambitious young man of his circumstance would be expected to attend, Noguchi entered Keio University, one of the oldest private colleges in Japan. There he studied Herbert Spencer and Thomas Carlyle, whose hero worship, in particular, made an impact on him. At the same time, he devoured such works as Washington Irving's *Sketch Book*, Oliver Goldsmith's "The Deserted Village," and Thomas Gray's "Elegy Written in a Country Churchyard." He even tried his hand at translating these eighteenth-century English poems into Japanese. On the other hand he did not ignore his native culture. His lifelong interest in haiku and Zen dates from this period, and the frequent visits he made to Zen temples while in college established a practice he continued later in his career in Japan.[1]

Though two years of college provided him with omnivorous reading in English, the young aspiring poet was not content with his education, for he had been dreaming of living and writing in an English-speaking country. In the last decade of the nineteenth century, Japanese immigration to the United States was at a beginning stage, so it was not difficult for a young man without technical skills to obtain a passport and visa. His initial plans were to look for some sort of employment near San Francisco, where he arrived in December 1893, with little money in his pocket, and to continue his studies.

For the next two years, he lived mainly among the Japanese immigrants in California. For almost a year he was employed by a Japanese-language newspaper in San Francisco, and he spent a great deal of time translating news of the Sino-Japanese War sent from Japan. As a Japanese patriot he was delighted to learn about the triumphant military campaign in China. Once, however, his industry and interests led him to walk from San Francisco as far as to Palo Alto, where he was able to live for several months at a prep school near the campus of Stanford University and to read Edgar Allan Poe's poems.[2] His continued reading of *Sketch Book*, particularly Irving's portrayal of life in England, inspired him to travel someday across the Atlantic.

The turning point of Noguchi's life in America came in 1896, when twenty-one years old and already an aspiring poet in English, he paid homage to the Western poet Joaquin Miller. Miller in turn admired Noguchi's youth and enthusiasm. Except for a few occasions, when Noguchi had to travel to Los Angeles partly on foot, or walk down the hills to see his publishers in San Francisco, he led a hermit's life for three years in Miller's mountain hut in Oakland. Through Miller he became acquainted with Edwin Markham, Dr. Charles Warren Stoddard, and the publishers Gelett Burgess and Porter Garnett.

Within a year of meeting Miller Noguchi published some of his earliest poems in three ephemeral journals of the day, *The Lark*, *The Chap Book*, and *The Philistine*. These poems attracted critical attention and in the following year he brought out his first collections of poetry, *Seen and Unseen or, Monologues of a Homeless Snail*, and *The Voice of the Valley*. These, too, received praise. Willa Cather, for instance, commenting on Yone Noguchi and Bliss Carman, the Canadian poet, wrote, "While Noguchi is by no means a great poet in the large, complicated modern sense of the word, he has more true inspiration, more melody from within than many a greater man" (Cather 2: 579). Despite initial success, however, his literary production became erratic and his fragile reputation was not sustained for long. Like the traditional wandering bard in Japan, the young Noguchi spent his energy walking and reading in the high mountains and in the fields. Of this experience he wrote in his journal, "I thank the rain, the most gentle rain of the Californian May, that drove me into a barn at San Miguel for two days and made me study 'Hamlet' line after line; whatever I know about it today is from my reading in that haystack" (*Japan and America* preface).

Later he traveled to Chicago, Boston, and New York, where, under the pseudonym Miss Morning Glory, he published a novella about a Japanese parlormaid.[3] After the turn of the century he journeyed to England, where he published his third volume of poetry in English, *From the Eastern Sea*. This collection stirred some interest among the English readers, especially Thomas Hardy and George Meredith. "Your poems," Meredith wrote to Noguchi, "are another instance of the energy, mysteriousness, and poetical feeling of the Japanese, from whom we are receiving much instruction" (*Japan and America* 111).

Yone Noguchi's wandering journey came to an end when he returned to Japan in 1904, the year his son Isamu was born and left behind in America with the mother. The elder Noguchi became a professor of English at Keio University in Tokyo, the same college from which he had withdrawn eleven years earlier. Among the more than ninety books he wrote in Japan, many of them in English, four are genuine collections of English poetry.[4] The rest ranges from books of literary and art criticism to travelogues. In the midst of his burgeoning literary career in Japan, he sometimes came back to America, and once visited England to deliver a lecture at Oxford's Magdalen College.

His role in East–West literary relations can scarcely be overestimated. The significance of his work should become even more evident when one tries to determine his influence on such major poets in Japan as Toson Shimazaki (1872–1943), Sakutaro Hagiwara (1886–1942), and Kotaro Takamura (1883–1956), as well as on W. B. Yeats, Ezra Pound, and Rabindranath Tagore, but most of all on the imagist poets of the day.

The standard explanation for the influences of Japanese poetry, especially haiku, on T. E. Hulme and Ezra Pound is that they studied Japanese poetics through the Harvard sinologist Ernest Fenollosa, who had a poor command of the Japanese language. However, since Noguchi's later poetry collected in *The Pilgrimage* and his literary criticism, *The Spirit of Japanese Poetry* in particular, were widely circulated, the standard explanation seems questionable. (A detailed discussion of the influences Noguchi's writings might have had on imagism will be given in Chapter 4.) Much more likely is the possibility that the imagists responded directly to the example of their fellow poet Noguchi. Acknowledging the books Noguchi had sent him, Pound in London wrote a letter to Noguchi in Japan on September 2, 1911:

> I had, of course, known of you, but I am much occupied with my mediaeval studies & had neglected to read your books altho' they lie with my own in Mathews shop & I am very familiar with the appearance of their covers.
>
> I am reading those you sent me but I do not yet know what to say of them except that they have delighted me . . . . You are giving us the spirit of Japan, is it not? very much as I am trying to deliver from obscurity certain forgotten odours of Provence & Tuscany.

In response to Noguchi's earlier inquiries about Pound's views of art and criticism, Pound remarked:

> Of your country I know almost nothing—surely if the east and the west are ever to understand each other that understanding must come slowly & come first through the arts.
>
> There is some criticism in the "Spirit of Romance" & there will be some in the prefaces to the "Guido" and the "Arnaut." But I might be more to the point if we who are artists should discuss the matters of technique & motive between ourselves.

"Also if you should write about these matters," he added, "I would discuss your letters with Mr. Yeats and likewise my answers. I have not answered before because your letter & your books have followed me through America, France, Italy, Germany and have reached me but lately. Let me thank you again for sending them, and believe me."[5]

In the 1920s and 1930s, Noguchi was also the most well-known interpreter of Japanese visual arts in the West, especially in England. Beginning with *The Spirit of Japanese Art*, he published in English ten volumes with colorful illustrations dealing with traditionally celebrated painters, such as Hiroshige, Korin, Utamaro, Hokusai, and Harunobu. Yeats, whose interest in the *noh* play is well known, wrote a letter to Noguchi in Japan from Oxford on June 27, 1921:[6]

> Dear Noguchi:
>
> Though I have been so long in writing, your "Hiroshige" has given me the greatest pleasure. I take more and more pleasure from oriental art; find more and more that it accords with what I aim at in my own work . . . . All your painters are simple, like the writers of Scottish ballads or the inventors of Irish stories, but one feels that Orpen and John have relatives in the patent office who are conscious of being at the fore-front of time.

Greatly impressed by the Japanese paintings illustrated in Noguchi's books, Yeats commented on the relationships of art and life that underlie these paintings:

> I would be simple myself but I do not know how. I am always turning over pages like those you have sent me, hoping that in my old age I may discover how. I wish somehow Japanese would tell us all about the lives . . . their talk, their loves, their religion, their friends . . . of these painters . . . . A form of beauty scarcely lasts a generation with us, but it lasts with you for centuries. You no more want to change it than a pious man wants to change the Lord's Prayer . . . not unless we have infected you with our egotism.

Yeats closed his letter on a personal note: "I wish I had found my way to your country a year ago & were still there, for my own remains un[words blurred] as I dreaded that it would. I have not seen Galway for a long time now for I am warned that it is no place for wife and child" (*English Letters* 220–21).

Noguchi's reputation as a poet and a critic grew in the West through the early 1930s, but World War II severed his ties to the West just as his relationship to his son Isamu had been strained ever since his birth. "I am getting old," Yone Noguchi wrote his son after the war, "and feel so sad and awful with what happened in Japan."[7] In 1947, in the midst of the chaos and devastation brought about by the war, without quite accomplishing his mission as he had wished, he died in Japan. Literary history, however, would amply justify that Yone Noguchi had played the most important role in modern times as a poet and interpreter of the divergent cultures of the East and the West.

***

Like his famous sculptor son, Isamu Noguchi, Yone Noguchi evolved his own distinct style, which drew upon both Western and Eastern traditions. Noguchi's first book, *Seen and Unseen*, shows that he was initially inspired by Walt Whitman and Joaquin Miller. The affinity with nature, as reflected in these poems, is clearly derived from Japanese traditions, but the sweeping lines and his romanticized self, which abound in his poetry, are reminiscent of Whitman:

The flat-boarded earth, nailed down at night,
     rusting under the darkness:
The Universe grows smaller,
     palpitating against its destiny:
My chilly soul–center of the world–gives seat
     to audible tears—the songs of the cricket.
I drink the darkness of a corner of the Universe,
. . . .
I am as a lost wind among the countless atoms
     of high Heaven![8]

What unites the two men with different backgrounds is not only their style but their world vision. In "Song of Myself" Whitman includes under the name of Self body and soul, good and evil, man and woman. The conclusion of this section in the poem, where he introduces the concept of balance, is a lyrical passage that celebrates the ecstasy of love. Whitman writes, "Prodigal, you have given me love—therefore I to you give love! / O unspeakable passionate love" (*Complete Poetry* 39). After this lyrical outburst he declares, "I am not the poet of goodness only, I do not decline to be the poet of wickedness also

. . . / I moisten the roots of all that has grown." As the poet of balance, Whitman accepts both good and evil; because he moistens the roots of all that has grown, he can call himself "a kosmos" (*Complete Poetry* 40–41). Noguchi's kosmos in "My Universe" has similar manifestations:

The world is round; no-headed, no-footed,
        having no left side, no right side!
And to say *Goodness* is to say *Badness*:
And to say *Badness* is to say *Goodness*.
[. . . . .]
The greatest robber seems like saint:
The cunning man seems like nothing-wanted beast!
Who is the real man in the face of God?
One who has fame not known,
One who has Wisdom not applauded,
One who has Goodness not respected:
One who has n't loved Wisdom dearly,
One who has n't hated Foolishness strongly!

                                    (*Selected English Writings* 1: 72–73)

Like Whitman, Noguchi believes in monism, and his ultimate goal in writing poetry is to achieve the ecstasies of the self in nature. Many of his early poems thus abound in the image in which life flows in on the self and others in nature. While Whitman in "Song of Myself" reincarnates himself into a sentient quahog on the beach, Noguchi in "Seas of Loneliness" identifies himself with a lone quail:

Underneath the void-colored shade of the trees,
        my "self" passed as a drowsy cloud into Somewhere.
I see my soul floating upon the face of the deep,
        nay the faceless face of the deepless deep—
[. . . . .]
Alas, I, without wisdom, without foolishness,
        without goodness, without badness,—am
        like god, a negative god, at least!
Is that a quail? One voice out of the back-hill
        jumped into the ocean of loneliness

                                    (*Selected English Writings* 1: 67)

Though he became a different kind of nature poet after he returned to Japan, his later poems still bear out Whitman's influence. The last stanza of Noguchi's religious poem "By a Buddha Temple" reads:

Ah, through the mountains and rivers,
        Let thy vastness thrill like that of air;

I read thy word in the flash of a leaf,
    Thy mystery in the whisper of a grass.

(Selected English Writings 1: 19)

Grass, which both poets love, is perhaps the most common and universal image in nature poetry. Such a technique, however, not only reveals the poet's sincere admiration of nature, but also betrays his abhorrence of civilization. In "Song of Myself" Whitman declares his independence from "civilization," which is represented by "houses and rooms." He detests the perfumes that envelop the domestic atmosphere because the fragrance is artificially distilled; the outdoor atmosphere, he argues, "is not a perfume, it has no taste of the distillation, it is odorless" (*Complete Poetry* 25). One of the disappointments Noguchi felt on his return to Japan was the rise of commercialism he witnessed. The beauty of the seashores near Tokyo was often marred by "the bathing crowd." But after summer, "with the autumn mellow and kind, the season of the clearest sky and softest breeze" (*Selected English Writings* 1: 19), he was able to recapture what Whitman called "Nature without check with original energy" (*Complete Poetry* 25):

Into the homelessness of the sea I awoke:
Oh, my heart of the wind and spray!
I am glad to be no-man to-day
With the laughter and dance of the sea-soul.[9]

(Selected English Writings 1: 142)

Noguchi's aversion to people, and to materialism in particular, originated from his mentor Joaquin Miller, "the Poet of the Sierras," as he called him. It was Miller who urged the fledgling poet to live "amid the roses, quite high above the cities and people." Noguchi pays Miller this compliment: "Never did I think Miller was particularly eccentric, never even once during my long stay with him; he was the most natural man; and his picturesqueness certainly was not a crime" (*Selected English Writings* 2: 228). Once Miller brought him a bunch of poppies ("The golden poppy is God's gold" is Miller's song), saying that they were the state flower. Then, he recalls, Miller's lecture followed:

> The sweetest flowers grow closest to the ground; you must not measure Nature by its size: if there is any measure, it will be that of beauty; and where is beauty there is truth. First of all, you must know Nature by yourself, not through the book. It would be ten thousand times better to know by your own knowledge the colour, the perfume and the beauty of a single tiny creeping vine in the valley than to know all the Rocky Mountains through a book; books are nothing. Read the history written on the brows of stars! (*Selected English Writings* 2: 229)

Such an attitude as Miller inspired in him led to the art of poetry that Noguchi practiced in his early work. Remembering Miller's oft-repeated statement, "My life is like the life of a bird," he tried in "Alone in the Canyon" to relive the life of a creature, or merge himself into the existence of a natural element:

"Good-bye my beloved family"—I am to-night
        buried under the sheeted coldness:
The dark weights of loneliness make me immovable!
Hark! the pine-wind blows,—blows!
Lo, the feeble, obedient leaves flee down to the ground
        fearing the stern-lipped wind voices!
Alas, the crickets' flutes, to-night, are broken!
The homeless snail climbing up the pillow,
        stares upon the silvered star-tears on my eyes!
The fish-like night-fogs flowering with mystery
        on the Bare-limbed branches:—
[..]

                                        (*Selected English Writings* 1: 67)

Far from being sentimentalized, a human being's harsh plight in nature is underscored by the images of coldness: the frozen ground, the blowing pine wind, the falling leaves, the crying crickets, the slowly climbing snail, the silvered stars above, the mysterious night fogs. This transformation of humanity into nature enables Noguchi in "To an Unknown Poet" to pose the following question: "When I am lost in the deep body of the mist on the hill, / the world seems built with me as its pillar! / Am I the god upon the face of the deep, deepless deepness in the Beginning?" (*Selected English Writings* 1: 61–62). In both poems Noguchi is speculating about the spiritual and transcendental power of humanity; conceptually, at least, he is uniting the will of a human being with the spirit of nature.

What Noguchi learned at the "Heights of the Sierras" was not only Miller's habit "to loaf and invite his own soul" in the presence of nature, a way of seeing nature, but also a way of experiencing love. For Noguchi, Miller was "the singer of 'a brother soul in some sweet bird, a sister spirit in a rose,' not the maker of loud-voiced ballads like the tide of a prairie fire or the marches of the Sierra mountains, but the dove-meek poet of love and humanity which . . . grow best and sweetest in silence" (*Selected English Writings* 2:232). It is revealing that Noguchi's autobiography, written in Japan years later, reprints Miller's favorite poem on silence:

Aye, Silence seems some maid at prayer,
God's arm about her when she prays
And where she prays and everywhere,

On storm-strewn days or sundown days—
What ill to Silence can befall
Since Silence knows no ill at all?

Vast silence seems some twilight sky
That learns as with her weight of stars
To rest, to rest, no more to roam,
But rest and rest eternally.
She loosens and lets down the bars,
She brings the kind-eyed cattle home,
She breathes the fragrant field of hay
And heaven is not far away.

(*Selected English Writings* 2: 232)

Many of Noguchi's poems, written both under the tutelage of Miller and later in Japan, echo Miller's ideas and methods of writing. In "My Poetry" (1897) Noguchi writes,

My Poetry begins with the tireless songs of the cricket,
      on the lean gray haired hill, in sober-faced evening.
And the next page is Stillness—
And what then, about the next to that?
Alas, the god puts his universe-covering hand over its sheets!
"Master, take off your hand for the humble servant!"
Asked in vain:—
How long for my meditation?

(*Selected English Writings* 1: 65)

"Bird of Silence" (1909) deals with the same theme:

Lonely ghost away from laughter and life,
Wing down, I welcome thee,
From the skies of thoughts and stars,
Bird of Silence, mystery's brother, as white
And aloof as is mystery,
Tired of humanity and of voice,
With thee, bird of Silence, I long to sail
Beyond the seas where Time and sorrows die,
[...]
I lost the voice as a willow spray
To whom a thrill is its golden song,
As a lotus whose break of cup
Is the sudden cry after aerial dance.

(*Selected English Writings* 1: 22)

In this piece the poet is preoccupied with the idea of silence, because silence is "whole and perfect." Silence in nature provides humanity with rest and happiness, creating a sense of eternity. Through silence, the poet implies, you are able to establish "your true friendship with the ghosts and the beautiful . . . . You have to abandon yourself to the beautiful only to create the absolute beauty and grandeur that makes this our human world look trifling." Through imagination, then, you can achieve "true love, when the reality of the external world ceases to be a standard, and you yourself will be a revelation, therefore a great art itself, of hope and passion which will never fail."[10]

The theme of silence in Noguchi's poetry is, furthermore, related to that of death and eternity. In "Eternal Death" (1897) death is treated as if it were alive: "a thief . . . with long and dusty beard," "the poetry-planted garden of silence," "the pearl-fruited orchard of meditation," "the song of my heart strings." To Noguchi, life and death are but two phases of the human soul; death is as much "a triumph to me" as life (*Selected English Writings* 1: 71). "The real poetry," Noguchi once stated, "should be accidental and also absolute" (*Japan and America* 98). Such a poem as "Eternal Death" captures the exact circumstances where the natural phenomena reveal both meanings of the accidental and the absolute. His method is, indeed, akin to that of great Japanese poets who write only of isolated aspects of nature but sing mainly of infinity from their accidental revelation.

***

Although Noguchi owes his poetry to Whitman and Miller, one cannot overlook the Japanese poetics that underlies much of his work. The most obvious tie can be found in its subject matter. Just as Japanese haiku do not treat such subjects as physical love, sex, war, beasts, earthquakes, and floods, Noguchi's poems shun eroticism, ugliness, hate, evil, and untruth. Unlike some poets in the West, Japanese poets abhor sentimentalism, romance, and vulgarity. "The Japanese poetry," Noguchi cautions, "is that of the moon, stars, and flowers, that of a bird and waterfall for the noisiest" (*Spirit of Japanese Poetry* 18–19). Japanese poets' way of avoiding the negative aspects of life, such as illness, is best illustrated by the haiku Basho wrote at his deathbed:

Lying ill on journey
Ah, my dreams
Run about the ruins of fields.[11]

(Basho, *Selected English Writings* 2: 70)

Japanese poetry is focused on nature because, as Noguchi says, "we human beings are not merely a part of Nature, but Nature itself" (*Selected English*

Writings 2: 59). To be sure, this is pantheism; he is accepting humanity and nature as a whole and leaving them as they are. But more importantly he is suggesting that Japanese poets always go to nature to make human life meaningful, to make "humanity more intensive." They share an artistic susceptibility where, as Noguchi writes, "the sunlight falls on the laughter of woods and waters, where the birds sing by the flowers" (*Selected English Writings* 2: 68–69). This mystical affinity between humanity and nature, between the beauty of love and the beauty of natural phenomena, is best stated in this verse by Noguchi:

It's accident to exist as a flower or a poet;
A mere twist of evolution but from the same force:
I see no form in them but only beauty in evidence;
It's the single touch of their imagination to get the
        embodiment of a poet or a flower:
To be a poet is to be a flower,
To be the dancer is to make the singer sing.[12]

(Noguchi, *Selected English Writings* 2: 69)

The fusion of humanity and nature, and the intensity of love and beauty with which it occurs, can be amply seen in haiku, as noted earlier. Noguchi regards Kikaku's haiku on the autumn moon as exemplary: "Autumn's full moon: / Lo, the shadows of a pine tree / Upon the mats!"[13] The beauty of the moonlight in Kikaku's haiku is not only humanized since the moonlight shines on the human-made object, but also intensified by the shadows of an intricate pine tree on the mats. Noguchi himself unifies an image of humanity and that of nature in his own work. "Lines" (1909) begins with this verse:

The sun I worship,
Not for the light, but for the shadows of the trees he draws:
Oh shadows welcome like an angel's bower,
Where I build Summer-day dreams!
Not for her love, but for the love's memory,

The poem ends on another suggestion of paradox:

To a bird's song I listen,
Not for the voice, but for the silence following after the song:
O Silence fresh from the bosom of voice!—
Melody from the Death-Land whither my face does ever turn!

(Noguchi, *Selected English Writings* 1: 152)

As Kikaku unifies the images of the moonlight and the mats, Noguchi unifies those of the sun and the love, the bird and the poet. Through the paradox of union both poets express the affinity of humanity and nature while at the same time maintaining an individual's separate identity and autonomy.

The most important tradition by which Noguchi's poetry is influenced is that of Zen. Zen practice calls for the austerity of the human mind; one should not allow one's individuality to control one's actions. "Drink tea when you are thirsty," says Noguchi, "eat food in your hunger. Rise with dawn, and sleep when the sun sets. But your trouble will begin when you let desire act freely; you have to soar above all personal desire" (*Story of Noguchi* 242). Zen does not recognize human reality, the existence of good and evil, because it is but the creation of one's will rather than the spirit of nature. The aim of the Zen poet, therefore, is to understand the spirit of nature. Observing the silent rites of a Zen priest, Noguchi once wrote, "Let the pine tree be green, and the roses red. We have to observe the mystery of every existence . . . . The language of silence cannot be understood by the way of reason, but by the power of impulse, which is abstraction" (*Story of Noguchi* 231–32).

To demonstrate the state of Zen, he composed a three-stanza poem, "By the Engakuji Temple: Moon Night," when he visited the Zen temple. The first two stanzas read,

Through the breath of perfume,
(O music of musics!)
Down creeps the moon
To fill my cup of song
With memory's wine.

Across the song of night and moon,
(O perfume of perfumes!)
My soul, as wind
Whose heart's too full to sing,
Only roams astray . . .[14]

(Noguchi, *Selected English Writings* 1: 136)

The poet's motivation for the union with nature, represented by the fragrance of the atmosphere and the moonlight, does not stem from his knowledge or desire. It is not the poet who is filling his "cup of song," but the moon that is creeping down. In the second stanza the poet reaches the state of Zen where, giving himself, he enters wholly into his actions—"the song of night and moon." That his soul is roaming astray suggests that he is giving up the ego. The loss of individuality within the union with nature is a condition of what R. H. Blyth calls, as noted earlier, "absolute spiritual poverty in which, having nothing, we possess all" (*Haiku* 162).

In haiku, there is little division between the perceiver and the perceived, spirit and matter, humanity and nature. "In the realm of poetry," Noguchi maintains, "there is no strict boundary between the domains generally called subjective and objective; while some *Hokku* poems appear to be objective, those poems are again by turns quite subjective through the great virtue of the writers having the fullest identification with the matter written on" (*Selected English Writings* 2: 73). Noguchi's poem "The Passing of Summer" (1909) reads:

An empty cup whence the light of passion is drunk!—
To-day a sad rumour passes through the trees,
A chill wind is borne by the stream,
The waves shiver in pain;
Where now the cicada's song long and hot?

(Noguchi, Selected English Writings 1: 149)

Such images as the chilly wind and the shivering waves are not used to signal the passing of summer. Rather the chilly wind and the shivering waves themselves constitute the passing of summer. Similarly, such phrases as "the light of passion" and "the cicada's song long and hot" are not metonymies of summer, thereby expressing nostalgia or some sort of sentiment about summer; instead they are the summer itself. In Noguchi's poetry, then, as in classic haiku, poetry and sensation are spontaneously joined in one and the same, so that there is scarcely any room left for rationalism or moralism.

Not all of Noguchi's English poems adhere to Japanese traditions. Most of his early poems, collected in *Seen and Unseen* and *The Voice of the Valley*, are beautiful expressions of the young poet's delight in his dreams, reveries, and mysteries about nature, the high Sierras, where he actually spent his life as a recluse. But the relationship of humanity to nature that he creates in his early work is quite different from that of his later work. The ecstasies of the self in nature he described in his early poetry are sometimes overindulgent, and this dependency of the self on nature results in a loss of equilibrium between them. Speaking of the same experience, Whitman cautions his own senses: "You villain touch! . . . / Unclench your floodgates, you are too much for me" (*Complete Poetry* 46). Unlike Whitman, however, the young Noguchi is at times unable to resist an urge toward overstatement and crude symbolism. In his poem "In the Valley," for example, the reveries of nature are most appropriately represented in terms of "the Sierra-rock, a tavern for the clouds" and "the Genii in the Valley-cavern." Man's will and desire, on the other hand, are alluded to by such prosaic expressions as "Fame" and "Gold"; "Heaven" and "mortals" are merely equated with "Glory" and "Decay" (*Selected English Writings* 1: 81–82).

Such a poem as "In the Valley" smacks of didacticism and moralism. It is not these qualities in his early poetry that attracted critics' attention. It is, to use his editor's phrase, "this unconventional child of nature . . . whose heart and soul lie naked and bare . . . . If he is sometimes obscure, it is because he had flown into cloud-land, where obscurity is a virtue."[15] Noguchi himself believed in the virtue of obscurity and indefiniteness in poetry and in art. To show this characteristic he quotes the English translation of a haiku found in an anthology:

Thought I, the fallen flowers
Are returning to their branch
But lo! they are butterflies.

Noguchi can only say that if this poem "means anything, it is the writer's ingenuity perhaps in finding a simile; but I wonder where is its poetical charm when it is expressed thus definitely" (*Selected English Writings* 2: 115–16).

What Noguchi strove to accomplish in his poetry, particularly in his later career, was to perceive a harmonious relationship between humanity and nature. For him the aim of poetry is not only to achieve the union of human-kind and nature, but also to maintain the identity of each within that union. The poet's chief function is not to express the feelings of human beings by the spirits of nature. This is analogous to what Noguchi saw in the print *Autumnal Moon at Tamagawa* by Hiroshige, an eminent nineteenth-century Japanese landscape painter, in which the moon over the river, the low mountain ranges in the background, and the fishermen engaged in night work are all harmoni-ously blended into a whole picture. Hiroshige in this painting, as Noguchi realizes, is not attempting to imitate nature or to make a copy whereby "the artist may become a soft-voiced servant to nature . . . not a real lover who truly understands her inner soul" (*Selected English Writings* 2: 184).

To sum up, Noguchi's poetry and criticism demonstrate that, in providing expression for nature, the artist must not express his or her own thought and logic. When Wordsworth sings, "I wandered, lonely as a cloud," he is simply feeling akin to the cloud rather than imposing the human will upon the will of nature. Similarly, in Noguchi's successful poems humans' position in nature becomes neither subordinate nor obtrusive, and both worlds can maintain a sense of dignity and autonomy.

NOTES

1. Much of Yone Noguchi's biographical information is found in the autobio-graphical essays written in English and in Japanese. The most useful is a collection of such essays titled *The Story of Yone Noguchi Told by Himself* (London: Chatto & Windus, 1914).

2. That Poe's poems made a great impact on the aspiring poet from Japan is indicated by the close similarity in a certain part of "Lines," one of Noguchi's

early poems in English, and Poe's "Eulalie." See "Lines," in *Pilgrimage* 2: 79; and "Eulalie," Poe, *Complete Works of Poe* 1: 121–22. When Noguchi's poems, including "Lines," appeared in *The Lark*, *The Chap Book*, and *The Philistine*, in 1896, he was accused of plagiarism by some critics while he was defended by his friends. Noguchi later refuted it in *Story of Yone Noguchi* 18. About this controversy, see Don B. Graham, "Yone Noguchi's 'Poe Mania,'" *Markham Review* 4 (1974): 58–60.

3. *The American Diary of a Japanese Girl* was published by Frank Leslie Publishing House, New York, in 1901 and also by Frederick A. Stokes Company, New York, in 1902. Both editions are illustrated in color and black and white by Genjiro Yeto. This book was later expanded into a full novel under the same title. Cf. *The American Diary of a Japanese Girl* (Tokyo: Fuzanbo and London: Elkin Mathews, 1902). This novel has recently been republished: Yone Noguchi, *The Diary of a Japanese Girl*, eds. Edward Marx and Laura E. Franey, with original illustrations by Genjiro Yeto (Philadelphia: Temple University Press, 2007).

4. The most comprehensive, though often inaccurate, bibliography of Yone Noguchi's writings in Japanese and in English is included in Usaburo Toyama, ed., *Essays on Yone Noguchi*, vol. 1. (Tokyo: Zokei Bijutsu Kyokai, 1963).

5. See Noguchi, *Collected English Letters*, ed. Ikuko Atsumi (Tokyo: Yone Noguchi Society, 1975), 210–11.

6. Yone Noguchi had earlier met Yeats in London, where *From the Eastern Sea* was published in 1903. In a letter of February 24, 1903, to his wife Leonie Gilmour he wrote, "I made many a nice young, lovely, kind friend among literary *geniuses* (attention!). W. B. Yeats or Lawrence Binyon, Moore and Bridges. They are so good; they invite me almost everyday. They are jolly companions. Their hairs are not long, I tell you" (*English Letters* 106).

7. See Isamu Noguchi, *Sculptor's World* (New York: Harper & Row, 1968), 31.

8. See Yone Noguchi, "The Invisible Night," *Seen and Unseen* 21. The poem first appeared in *The Lark*. The poem is quoted from *Selected English Writings* 1: 65.

9. See "At the Yuigahama Shore by Kamakura," *Pilgrimage* 1: 34. The poem is reprinted in Noguchi's travelogue *Kamakura* 38–39.

10. See *Story of Noguchi* 223–24. Noguchi discusses elsewhere what is to him the true meaning of realism: "While I admit the art of some artist which has the detail of beauty, I must tell him that reality, even when true, is not the whole thing; he should learn the art of escaping from it. That art is, in my opinion, the greatest of all arts; without it, art will never bring us the eternal and the mysterious" (Yone Noguchi, *Spirit of Japanese Art* [New York: Dutton, 1915], 103).

11. Quoted, in Noguchi's translation, in *Spirit of Japanese Poetry* 38.

12. Quoted in *Spirit of Japanese Poetry* 37. This particular poem, however, cannot be found in any of Noguchi's poetry collections.

13. Quoted, in Noguchi's translation, in Noguchi, *Through the Torii* (Boston: Four Seas, 1922), 132.

14. See "By the Engakuji Temple: Moon Night," *Pilgrimage* 1: 5. The Engakuji Temple, located in Kamakura, an ancient capital of Japan, was founded in the thirteenth century by Tokimune Hojo, hero of the feudal government, who was a great believer in Zen Buddhism.

15. See Charles Warren Stoddard, "Introduction," *Voice of Valley* 10–11.

Chapter 4

Ezra Pound, Imagism, and Haiku

It is commonplace to say that imagism played a crucial role in poetic modernism, and that Ezra Pound, more than anyone else, put this poetics to practice in the 1910s. Yet imagism still remains a somewhat cloudy topic. Many discussions content themselves with restatements of Pound's celebrated essay on vorticism, published in September 1914 ("Vorticism" 461–71). Even Hugh Kenner, the most eminent critic of Pound, says, "The history of the Imagist Movement is a red herring." He admonishes one "to keep one's eyes on Pound's texts, and avoid generalities about Imagism" (Kenner 58).

In the "Vorticism" essay, Pound acknowledged for the first time in his career his indebtedness to the spirit of Japanese poetry in general and the technique of *hokku*, an older term of haiku, in particular. Among the Poundians, and there have been many in the East and in the West, who have tried to reconstruct the historical set of circumstances in which Pound moved, Earl Miner gives the best account of the profound influences that Japanese poetry had on the early Pound's early poetry. It is Miner who offers the best annotated evidence that the sources for Pound's interest in Japanese poetics were partly provided by Pound's fellow imagists such as T. E. Hulme, F. S. Flint, and Richard Aldington.[1]

It is Miner as well who most frequently comments on the role Yone Noguchi played in the introduction and interpretation of Japanese poetry to the English audience during the early decades of the twentieth century.[2] As noted earlier, Noguchi was indeed a well-known bilingual Japanese and American poet, who by 1915 had published not only books of criticism widely read in England and America (*The Spirit of Japanese Poetry* and *The Spirit of Japanese Art*), but also several collections of his own English poems. By this date, as noted earlier, his poems had been praised by Willa Cather, Joaquin Miller, and Gelett Burgess in America, by Bliss Carman in Canada, and by

George Meredith, William Rossetti, Thomas Hardy, and others in England. What is surprising, therefore, is Miner's dismissive treatment of Noguchi's English writings as having had little to do with the imagist movement and with Pound in particular.

***

As Pound explained in his essay, the image is not a static, rational idea: "It is a radiant node or cluster; it is what I can, and must perforce, call a VORTEX, from which, and through which, and into which ideas are constantly rushing. In decency one can only call it a VORTEX. And from this necessity came the name 'vorticism'" ("Vorticism" 469–70). "A year later Pound defined the form of an image by stating that the image "may be a sketch, a vignette, a criticism, an epigram or anything else you like. It may be impressionism, it may even be very good prose" ("As for Imagisme" 349). An image, he argued, does not constitute simply a picture of something. As a vortex, the image must be "endowed with energy" ("As for Imagisme" 349). Imagism, in turn, is likened to the painter's use of pigment. "The painter," Pound wrote, "should use his colour because he sees it or feels it. I don't much care whether he is representative or non-representative . . . . It is the same in writing poems, the author must use his *image* . . . not because he thinks he can use it to back up some creed or some system of ethics or economics" ("Vorticism" 464).

To demonstrate his poetic theory, Pound thought of an image not as a decorative emblem or symbol but as a seed capable of germinating and developing into another organism. As an illustration he presented what he called "a *hokku*-like sentence" he had written:

The apparition of these faces in the crowd:
        Petals, on a wet, black bough.

"In a poem of this sort," he explained, "one is trying to record the precise instant when a thing outward and objective transforms itself, or darts into a thing inward and subjective" ("Vorticism" 467). The image of the faces in the crowd is based in immediate experience at a metro station in Paris; it was "a thing outward and objective." Not only did Pound actually see the "thing," but it generated such a sensation that he could not shake it out of his mind. This image, he emphasizes, "transforms itself, or darts into a thing inward and subjective," that is, the image of the "Petals, on a wet, black bough." Imagism is further contrasted to symbolism: "The symbolist's *symbols* have a fixed value, like numbers in arithmetic, like 1, 2, and 7. The imagiste's images have a variable significance, like the signs *a*, *b*, and *x* in algebra" ("Vorticism" 463).

Although Pound's definition is clear enough, the sources for his ideas are hard to determine. Most discussions about the genesis of the imagist movement are speculative at best. Pound's insistence that an image in poetry must be active rather than passive suggests that a poem is not a description of something, but, as Aristotle had said of tragedy, an action. Pound approaches Aristotelianism in his insistence that the image of the faces in the crowd in his metro poem was not simply a description of his sensation at the station, but an active entity capable of dynamic development. According to his experience, this particular image instantly transformed itself into another image, that of the petals on a wet, black bough. To Pound the success of this poem resulted from his instantaneous perception of the relatedness between the two entirely different objects.

But Pound's note on the genesis of "In a Station of the Metro" in the "Vorticism" essay makes it clear that there was nothing instantaneous about the composition of this poem. It was in 1911 that Pound, having seen those "beautiful faces" at La Concorde, wrote a thirty-line poem, "and destroyed it because it was what we call work 'of second intensity'" ("Vorticism" 467). Six months later he reduced the longer text to a poem half the length, and still a year later he wrote the final version, a two-line poem. Pound's insistence on the instantaneous perception of the metro images drove him to repeated attempts at recreating the instantaneous images he had perceived a year-and-a-half earlier. Traditionally, the principle of instantaneity and spontaneity is as fundamental for the composition of haiku as the same principle is when applied to Zen-inspired painting and calligraphy. In any event, his discovery of *hokku* in 1913 to 1914 was, as he says, "useful in getting out of the impasse in which I had been left by my metro emotion" ("Vorticism" 467). To Pound, the most important thing he learned about *hokku* was "this particular sort of consciousness," which he was unable to identify with any version of impressionist art.[3]

Another equally important tenet of imagism calls for directness in expression. The immediate model for this principle was nineteenth-century French prose. Pound did not mention specific English poets but seemed adamantly opposed to Victorian poetry, which he characterized as wordy and rhetorical. Instead he urged his fellow poets "to bring poetry up to the level of prose." "Flaubert and De Maupassant," he believed, "lifted prose to the rank of a finer art, and one has no patience with contemporary poets who escape from all the difficulties of the infinitely difficult art of good prose by pouring themselves into loose verses" ("Vorticism" 462).

If Pound's ideal poetry has the directness and clarity of good prose as opposed to the suggestiveness and vagueness of symbolist poetry, then his sources did not include Yeats. Even though Yeats dedicated the *noh* play *At the Hawk's Well* to Pound, Yeats was not enthusiastic about Pound's poetics.

"My own theory of poetical or legendary drama," Yeats wrote to Fiona Macleod, "is that it should have no realistic, or elaborate, but only a symbolic and decorative setting. A forest, for instance, should be represented by a forest pattern and not by a forest painting" (Sharp 280–81). The difference between Pound and Yeats reveals itself in the two poets' differing views of the Japanese *noh* play.

This disagreement between Pound and Yeats over whether poetic images should be suggestive or active also involves what Noguchi, a poet and critic well acquainted with both poets, felt compelled to write in "What Is a Hokku Poem?" published in London in 1913.[4] In that essay, Noguchi first defined *hokku* as an expression of Japanese poets' "understanding of Nature," or, better put, as a song or chant of "their longing or wonder or adoration toward Mother Nature" that is "never mystified by any cloud or mist like Truth or Beauty of Keats' understanding." Noguchi differentiated between the "suggestive" and subjective coloration of English poetry and the Japanese *hokku*, "distinctly clear-cut like a diamond or star." He argued, "I say that the star itself has almost no share in the creation of a condition even when your dream or vision is gained through its beauty. . . . I value the 'hokku' poem, at least some of them, because of its own truth and humanity simple and plain." Noguchi then analyzed the aim of *hokku*: the *hokku* poet expresses the spirit of nature rather than the will of man or woman. Noguchi would agree that *hokku* is "suggestive" only if the word *suggestive* means that "truth and humanity are suggestive." He added, "But I can say myself as a poet . . . that your poem would certainly end in artificiality if you start out to be suggestive from the beginning" ("What Is a Hokku Poem?" 355).

Finally, Noguchi based his definition and analysis of aim in Zen philosophy, understood as discipline of the mind: one should not allow one's individuality to control action. Indeed, Zen does not recognize human reality, the existence of good and evil, because this reality is the creation of human will rather than the spirit of nature. Noguchi thus observed that "there is no word in so common use by Western critics as suggestive, which makes more mischief than enlightenment." Although Western critics "mean it quite simply . . . to be a new force or salvation, . . . I say that no critic is necessary for this world of poetry" ("What Is a Hokku Poem?" 355).

By 1918, Pound's vorticist theory had extended to his discussion of Chinese characters. As the correspondence between Pound and Mary Fenollosa, widow of Ernest Fenollosa, indicates, Pound began to receive Fenollosa's manuscripts as early as 1913.[5] Fenollosa's essay "The Chinese Written Characters as a Medium of Poetry," posthumously published by Pound in *The Little Review* in 1918, attempted to show that Chinese characters, which Pound called ideograms, derive from visual rather than aural experiences. A Chinese character, Fenollosa noted, signifies an observable action instead of an abstract notion. Unlike a Western word, a phonetic sign, the Chinese character denotes a concrete, natural phenomenon. It, Fenollosa wrote, "is based upon a vivid shorthand picture of the operations of nature. In the algebraic figure and in the spoken word there is no natural connection between thing and sign: all depends upon sheer convention. But the Chinese method follows natural suggestion" (*Chinese Characters* 8).

Pound's attempt to verify Fenollosa's theory involved not only his contemporaries, poets and critics living in London in the 1910s, but his own effort to search for ideas in other sources. One of these sources was the Japanese *noh* play, in which Pound became interested through Fenollosa's notes. It is generally understood that Pound's interest in Japanese poetry, especially *hokku*, grew partly through his acquaintance with Fenollosa's writings. None of Fenollosa's writings, however, directly concerns Japanese poetry, let alone *hokku*. Having lived many years in Japan as an art critic, Fenollosa became well versed in Japanese art and literature, but his actual knowledge of the Japanese language was not profound.[6] It is, therefore, inconceivable that Pound became well acquainted with *hokku* through Fenollosa. It is also unlikely that English contemporaries such as T. E. Hulme and F. S. Flint, who are said to have introduced *hokku* to Pound, served his purpose. Pound would not have been able to learn from them the subtle elements of Japanese poetry because they themselves did not have firsthand knowledge of the Japanese language.[7]

***

Pound's most likely source of information was Noguchi, as noted earlier. He first corresponded with Pound and then met Pound, along with Yeats, when he gave a series of lectures on Japanese poetry in England in early 1914. The relationship between Pound and Noguchi began in 1911, when Noguchi sent his fifth collection of English poems, *The Pilgrimage* (1908 and 1909) in two volumes, to Pound with a note: "As I am not yet acquainted with your work, I wish you [would] send your books or books which you like to have me read. This little note may sound quite businesslike, but I can promise you that I can do better in my next letter to you." Noguchi also wrote as a postscript, "I am anxious to read not only your poetical work but also your criticism" (Kodama 4). Pound acknowledged receipt of the books and note and thanked him in a letter postmarked September 2, 1911. Pound further wrote, in part, "You are giving us the spirit of Japan, is it not? very much as I am trying to deliver from obscurity certain forgotten odours of Provence & Tuscany . . . . Of your country I know almost nothing—surely if the east & the west are ever to understand each other that understanding must come slowly & come first through the arts . . . . But I might be more to the point if we who are artists should discuss the matters of technique & motive between ourselves. Also if you should write about these matters I would discuss your letters with Mr. Yeats and likewise my answers" (*English Letters* 210–11).

Although Noguchi did not write again to Pound, Noguchi published his essay "What Is a Hokku Poem?" in London in January 1913, as noted earlier. In the meantime three books of criticism by Noguchi appeared during this period: *The Spirit of Japanese Poetry* (1914), *Through the Torii* (1914), and *The Spirit of Japanese Art* (1915). Noguchi was also invited to contribute "The Everlasting Sorrow: A Japanese Noh Play" in 1917 and an article, "The Japanese Noh Play," in 1918 to *The Egoist*.[8] Pound's encouragement was perhaps responsible for the publication of some of Noguchi's own haiku in *The Egoist* and in *Poetry*.

Because his essays and lectures during this period also dealt with Japanese art, Yeats, who was interested in Japanese painting and the *noh* play became interested in Noguchi's work as well.[9] As Pound's and Yeats's letters to Noguchi indicate, Pound and Yeats not only were close associates themselves but also were both well acquainted with Noguchi. Despite the active dialogues that occurred between Pound and Noguchi, critics have not seriously considered their relationship. The only critic who has mentioned Noguchi in discussing the imagist movement regarded Noguchi not as a poet and critic from whose ideas Pound might have benefited, but as one of the poets whom Pound himself influenced (Goodwin 32). Such a preposterous connection is undermined by the simple fact that most of Noguchi's English poems, as Pound noted in his letter to Noguchi, had been published in America and England long before the early 1910s, when Pound and his fellow poets began to discuss imagism among themselves. It is more accurate historically to say that Noguchi influenced Pound rather than the other way around.

Pound had apparently known little about Japanese poetry before he attended the April 1909 meeting of the Poets' Club. This group, headed by T. E. Hulme, was succeeded by another group called "*Les Imagistes*," or "*Des Imagistes*," which Pound led from 1912 to 1914.[10] Although Pound in fact joined the Poets' Club, its sessions did not prove of much inspiration to him. Richard Aldington, who joined in 1911, was more interested in the color prints by Utamaro, Hokusai, and others found in the British Museum than in Japanese poetry.[11] The fact that Pound was more seriously interested in Japanese poetry than was Aldington is indicated by a parody of Pound's metro poem that Aldington published in the January 1915 issue of *The Egoist*.[12] Allen Upward, another member of "*Les Imagistes*" group, whom Pound had met in 1911, had some importance for Pound because Upward used the term "whirl-swirl" in his book *The New Word* (1908). Upward, a self-styled intellectual and a poet, had "a powerful and original mind clearly and trenchantly concerned with matters that bear directly on what Pound meant by 'vortex.'"[13] But Upward, who was well read in Confucius and perhaps familiar with Chinese poetry, did not have sufficient knowledge of Japanese poetry, let alone of *hokku*, to influence Pound (Harmer 38).

The degree of Pound's initial interest in *hokku*, therefore, was not entirely clear, for he was much occupied with Provencal poetry and criticism, as his letter to Noguchi indicates. It is quite possible that Pound learned about *hokku* from T. E. Hulme and F. S. Flint, who were experimenting with *hokku* and *tanka*, the thirty-one-syllable Japanese poetic form (Miner, "Pound" 572). The difficulty with this assumption, however, is that Hulme and Flint studied *hokku* through French translators and critics who used the terms *haiku* and *haikai*, more modern words, rather than *hokku*. Most strikingly, neither Pound nor Noguchi referred to the Japanese poem as *haiku* or *haikai*; both consistently called it *hokku* in their writings.

However coincidental this might have been, there are two more pieces of evidence suggesting that Pound might have learned about *hokku* in Noguchi's work. First, as already observed, the essay "What Is a Hokku Poem?"—in which Noguchi declared that poetic images must be active instead of suggestive, direct instead of symbolic, and that the aim of a *hokku* is to understand the spirit of nature rather than to express the will of an individual—was published in *Rhythm* (London) in January 1913, almost two years before Pound's essay "Vorticism." Even Pound's essay "A Few Don'ts," the earliest manifesto on imagism, appeared in the March 1913 issue of *Poetry* (Chicago) two months after Noguchi's essay. Second, Noguchi's book of criticism, *The Spirit of Japanese Poetry*, was published in London by John Murray in March 1914, half a year before Pound's "Vorticism" essay.[14]

Moreover, the key chapter of Noguchi's book, titled "The Japanese Hokku Poetry," was a lecture delivered in the Hall of Magdalen College, Oxford, on January 28, 1914, at the invitation of Robert Bridges, the poet laureate, and T. H. Warren, president of the college and professor of poetry at the university. The first chapter, "Japanese Poetry," was also based on a lecture Noguchi gave at the Japan Society of London on January 14, 1914. The rest of the book had been presented as other lectures to such audiences as the Royal Asiatic Society and the Quest Society in England before April 1914, when Noguchi left London for Tokyo by way of Paris, Berlin, and Moscow. It is altogether possible that Pound heard Noguchi lecture at the Quest Society since Pound, Wyndham Lewis, and T. E. Hulme all lectured there in 1914.[15] During this stay in England, *Through the Torii*, another collection of essays that included a variety of commentary on William Rossetti, James Whistler, W. B. Yeats, and Oscar Wilde, and his autobiography, *The Story of Yone Noguchi Told by Himself*, also appeared in print.

It is most intriguing that Pound's "Vorticism" essay quoted a famous *hokku* by Arakida Moritake (1473–1549) just before discussing the often-quoted metro poem:

The fallen blossom flies back to its branch:
    A butterfly.

(Moritake, "Vorticism" 467)

This *hokku* in Japanese has three lines:

Rak-ka eda ni
Kaeru to mireba
Kocho-o kana

Noguchi translated this poem in three lines:

I thought I saw the fallen leaves
Returning to their branches:
Alas, butterflies were they.

(Moritake, *Spirit of Japanese Poetry* 50)

Pound must have reconstructed the *hokku* in two lines simply because he had in mind "a form of super-position" in which his metro poem was to be composed. The similarities between Pound's and Noguchi's versions of the poem in question do not seem coincidental, because the superpository division is indicated by a colon in both constructions. Both translations have identical key words: "fallen," "branch," and "butterfly." The only difference in diction is between Pound's "blossom" *(ka* in Japanese) and Noguchi's "leaves." In syntax, however, these translations are different: Noguchi's version is subjective from the start and ends objectively; the reverse is true in Pound's rendering. Syntactically, Noguchi's version is closer to the Japanese original than Pound's. A literal translation of Moritake's first two lines, "Rak-ka eda ni / Kaeru to mireba," would read: "The fallen blossom appears to come back to its branch."

What appealed to Pound was the terseness and intensity of imagery in a *hokku*. Irked by the decorative and superfluous style of much Victorian poetry, he urged his fellow poets to eliminate words that do not contribute to the central meaning of the poem. "All poetic language," Pound insisted, "is the language of exploration. Since the beginning of bad writing, writers have used images as ornaments" ("Vorticism" 466). By saying, "Great literature is simply language charged with meaning to the utmost possible degree," he meant to elaborate the imagist principle that using fewer words maximizes and intensifies meaning.[16] In "What Is a Hokku Poem?" Noguchi wrote, "I always thought that the most beautiful flowers grow close to the ground, and they need no hundred petals for expressing their own beauty; how can you call it real poetry if you cannot tell it by a few words?" (355).

Pound, furthermore, applied the principle of terseness and intensity to the construction of a single image in his poetry. "The 'one image poem,'" Pound noted, "is a form of super-position, that is to say it is one idea set on top of another. I found it useful in getting out of the impasse in which I had been left by my metro emotion" ("Vorticism" 467). Noguchi pointed out the same technique: "*Hokku* means literally a single utterance or the utterance of a single verse; that utterance should be like a 'moth light playing on reality's dusk,' or 'an art hung, as a web, in the air of perfume,' swinging soft in music of a moment" (*Spirit of Japanese Poetry* 39). To illustrate his point, Noguchi quoted a haiku by Buson:

The night of the Spring,—
Oh, between the eve
And the dawn.

(Buson, Spirit of Japanese Poetry 39)

This haiku was placed against the opening passage of Makura no Soshi (*Pillow Sketches*) by Sei Shonagon (966?–1025?), a celebrated prose writer in medieval Japan: "I love to watch the dawn grow gradually white and whiter, till a faint rosy tinge crowns the mountain's crest, while slender streaks of purple cloud extend themselves above." Noguchi considered Buson's image far more vivid and intensive than Sei Shonagon's, remarking, "Buson is pleased to introduce the night of the Spring which should be beautiful without questioning, since it lies between those two beautiful things, the eve and the dawn" (*Spirit of Japanese Poetry* 48–49).

***

Not only was Noguchi an interpreter of *hokku* poems for the English reader, but he tried his hand at writing *hokku* poems in English. He later collected them in the volume *Japanese Hokkus* (1920), which he dedicated to Yeats.[17] One of Noguchi's earliest *hokku* is reminiscent of Buson's, quoted above:

Tell me the street to Heaven.
This? Or that? Oh, which?
What webs of streets!

(Noguchi, "What Is a Hokku Poem?" 358)

He wrote this *hokku* in England, he says, "when I most abruptly awoke in 1902 to the noise of Charing Cross. . . . And it was by Westminster Bridge where I heard the evening chime that I wrote again in 'hokku' which appears, when translated, as follows" ("What Is a Hokku Poem?" 358):

Is it, Oh, list:
The great voice of Judgment Day?
So runs Thames and my Life.

(Noguchi, "What Is a Hokku Poem?")

Noguchi wrote many *hokku*-like poems like these in imitation of the Japanese *hokku*, as did Pound. The superpository technique, which Pound said he had discovered in Japanese *hokku*, resembles that of Noguchi. For instance, Pound's "Alba," typical of his many *hokku*-like poems, reads,

As cool as the pale wet leaves
of lily-of-the-valley
She lay beside me in the dawn.

(Pound, *Personae* 109)

Most of Noguchi's *hokku*, as the two poems quoted above show, do have a form of superposition. Like Pound's, Noguchi's *hokku* constitutes one image poem which has two separate ideas set on top of one another. In the first poem by Noguchi, an idea of "the street to Heaven" is set on top of an idea of "webs," despite a close similarity between the two images. In the second, an idea of the flow of the Thames is set on top of an idea of the course of "my Life."

But there are some differences between Noguchi's and Pound's *hokku*. Noguchi does not as closely adhere to the well-established Japanese syllabic measure of five or seven as does Pound. Noguchi's two *hokku* above have 7-5-4 and 4-7-6 measures; Pound's "Alba," "Fan-Piece, for Her Imperial Lord," and "Ts'ai Chi'h" have those of 7-7-8, 7-5-7, and 8-7-7, respectively. If the first line of Pound's metro poem had been reconstructed as two lines, the poem would have had a measure of 5-7-7 ("The apparition / Of these faces in the crowd / Petals on a wet, black bough"), much like a Japanese *hokku*. Noguchi, moreover, tends to ignore the long-established poetic tradition in which a Japanese *hokku* has an explicit reference to a season. Pound, on the other hand, consciously adheres to this tradition as seen in many of his *hokku*-like poems and somewhat longer pieces such as "Heather" and "Society" (*Personae* 109–11).

What a Japanese *hokku* and Pound's image share besides their brevity and intensity is the poet's ability to escape the confinement of the poem. The sense of liberation in *hokku* is usually accomplished through references to time and space. A Japanese *hokku* contains not only a reference to a season, an indication of time, but an image of nature, that of space. Pound's *hokku*-like poems, such as "In a Station of the Metro" and "Alba," indeed have references to time and space. Pound called the metro emotion, which came from the image of the faces in the crowd, "a thing outward and objective," and the image of the petals, on a wet, black bough "a thing inward and subjective." The image of the petals, nevertheless, is a natural object in contrast to that of the faces in the crowded station, a human object.

In Pound's mind—in the realm of subjective perception—the image of the faces, an objective image, transforms into the image of the petals, a subjective image. This perception also means that the image of the faces, an image of people, transforms into that of the petals, an image of nature. The shifting of objective and subjective images in Pound's poem is depicted in terms of a vortex, in which an image is not only active in itself but also capable of merging into another image that appears in its wake. Because Pound's image has this tendency, it is often as difficult to separate the mental vision from the external as it is to separate mind from matter, the perceiver from the perceived, in Japanese *hokku*.

In *The Spirit of Japanese Poetry*, Noguchi is as critical as Pound of the Western poet's tendency to wordiness. Noguchi's emphasis on the Japanese *hokku* as "the real poetry of action" entails that a *hokku* aim to narrow the distance between humanity and nature, the perceiver and the perceived. The narrower the distance the better the *hokku* becomes. Based on "Lao Tze's canon of spiritual anarchism" and Zen's principle of controlling the mind, Noguchi declares:

> To attach too closely to the subject matter in literary expression is never a way to complete the real saturation; the real infinite significance will only be accomplished at such a consummate moment when the end and means are least noticeable, and the subject and expression never fluctuate from each other, being in perfect collocation; it is the partial loss of the birthright of each that gains an artistic triumph . . . . I do never mean that the *Hokku* poems are lyrical poetry in the general Western understanding; but the Japanese mind gets the effect before perceiving the fact of their brevity, its sensibility resounding to their single note, as if the calm bosom of river water to the song of a bird. (*Spirit of Japanese Poetry* 34)

To illustrate what he calls "the sense of mystical affinity between the life of Nature and the life of man, between the beauty of flowers and the beauty of love," he quotes his own poem, as discussed in Chapter 3 on Noguchi:

It's accident to exist as a flower or a poet:
A mere twist of evolution but from the same force;

I see no form in them but only beauty in evidence;

It's the single touch of their imagination to get the embodiment of a poet
or a flower:

To be a poet is to be a flower,
To be the dancer is to make the singer sing.

(Noguchi, *Spirit of Japanese Poetry* 37)[18]

Pound, on the other hand, views the affinity between humanity and nature dif-
ferently. What Pound calls "a thing inward and subjective" does not necessarily correspond to a vision of a person; nor is "a thing outward and objective"
the same thing as a vision of nature.

This fusion of humanity and nature is called spontaneity in Zen. The best
hokku poems, because of their linguistic limitations, are inwardly extensive
and outwardly infinite. A severe constraint imposed on one aspect of *hokku*
must be balanced by a spontaneous, boundless freedom on the other. From a
Zen point of view, such a vision is devoid of thought and emotion. Since Zen
is the most important philosophical tradition influencing Japanese *hokku*, the
hokku poet aims at understanding the spirit of nature. Basho, a Zen-inspired
poet, recognizes little division between humanity and nature, the subjective
and the objective; he is never concerned with the problems of good and evil.
Placed against this tradition, Pound's poetics in its philosophical aspect con-
siderably differs from Basho's. Pound cannot be called a Zen poet because
he declared: "An 'Image' is that which presents an intellectual and emotional
complex in an instant of time" (*Literary Essays* 4). A Zen poet seeks satori,
an enlightenment that transcends time and place, and even the consciousness
of self. This enlightenment is defined as a state absolutely free of any thought
or emotion, a state that corresponds to that of nature. For a Zen-inspired poet,
nature is a mirror of the enlightened self; one must see and hear things as they
really are by making one's consciousness pure and clear. Pound seems to be
able to appreciate this state of mind, but obviously he does not necessarily try
to seek it in his own work.

In fact, Japanese traditional haiku seldom take physical love, war, beasts,
earthquakes, floods, and the like for their subjects. And while Pound's poetry
does express good and evil, love and hatred, individual feeling and collective
myth, Basho's shuns such sentiments and emotions altogether. Pound and
a Zen poet, however, do agree that their poetic vision is spontaneous and
capable of attaining enlightenment. Pound maintained, "It is the presentation
of such a 'complex' instantaneously which gives that sense of sudden liberation; that sense of freedom from time and space limits; that sense of sudden
growth, which we experience in the presence of the greatest works of art"

(*Literary Essays* 4). Pound's observation, however, is very much a Western formulation of an experience familiar to Zen-inspired artists.

This sense of liberation suggests an impersonal conception of poetry, for it focuses attention not on the poet but on the image. T. S. Eliot, whom most observers agree Pound influenced, held the same view (*Selected Essays* 8–10). Japanese poets such as Basho, Buson, and Issa held the same principle. Their poetry seldom dealt with dreams, fantasies, or concepts of heaven and hell; it was strictly concerned with the portrayal of nature—mountains, trees, flowers, birds, animals, insects, waterfalls, nights, days, seasons. For the Japanese *hokku* poet, nature is a mirror of the enlightened self; the poet must see and hear things as they really are by making his or her consciousness pure, natural, and unemotional. "Japanese poets," Noguchi wrote, "go to Nature to make life more meaningful, sing of flowers and birds to make humanity more intensive" (*Spirit of Japanese Poetry* 37).

As opposed to his later poetry, Pound's early poetry, and his *hokku*-like poems in particular, have little to do with his personal emotion or thought. In such poetry, Pound is not really concerned with thought and emotion. If Pound's *hokku* sounded intellectual or emotional, it did so only to an English reader who was still Arnoldian in his or her taste and unfamiliar with the imagist movement of the 1910s, not to mention with "the spirit of Japanese poetry" Noguchi tried to introduce to the English audience. Japanese poetry shuns symbols and metaphors because figurative language might lessen the intensity and spontaneity of a newly experienced sensation. Such expressions would not only undermine originality in the poet's sensibility, but resort to intellectualization—as well as what Noguchi, perhaps echoing Matthew Arnold, called "a criticism Iof life," which traditionally Japanese poetry was not (*Through the Torii* 159).

The *hokku* poet may not only aim at expressing sensation but also at generalizing and hence depersonalizing it. This characteristic can be shown even by one of Basho's lesser-known *hokku*, as noted earlier:

How cool it is!
Putting the feet on the wall:
An afternoon nap.[19]

(Basho)

In "Alba" what Pound expressed was not the personal feeling he had about the woman lying beside him at dawn, but his spontaneous sensation of the coolness of "the pale wet leaves / of lily-of-the-valley." Likewise, the sensation of slowly cooling hot water was Pound's subject in "The Bath Tub," as the title suggests, rather than his feelings about the woman (*Personae* 100). The image of a "fan of white silk, / clear as frost on the grass-blade" is central in "Fan-Piece, for Her Imperial Lord," where a minimal image of the lord's concubine is evoked by a one-word reference to her: "You also are laid aside" (*Personae* 108). Such subtleties could not have been learned from Pound's fellow imagists like Flint and Aldington. These imagists remained labored, superficial imitators of Japanese *hokku*. Pound and Noguchi, by contrast, showed themselves far more capable of understanding the spirit of Japanese poetry.

***

As partly suggested in the previous remarks on superposition, the *hokku* also provided a structural model for Pound's version of imagism. Acknowledging that the Japanese had evolved this short form of poetry, Pound seized on the unique form of "super-position" which, he observed, constitutes a *hokku*. To him, the *hokku* often consists of two disparate images in juxtaposition, and yet it appears as a single image. Lacking the copula *is* or the preposition *like*, the image cannot be metaphoric or analogical. As Pound's account of the composition of the metro poem shows, he had no intention of likening the image of the beautiful faces in the crowd to the image of petals on a wet, black bough or of making one image suggestive or representative of the other.[20] If one image is used to suggest another or to represent another, both images would be weakened. But if one image is used to generate or intensify another, and the other image, in turn, intensifies the first one, then the whole poem as one image would be intensified.

The key to the superpository structure of Pound's image is a coalescence of two unlike images. Such an image must be generated "in an instant of time," as Pound cautions in his essay "A Few Don'ts" (*Literary Essays* 4). Creating such an image needs no preparations, no explanations, no qualifications; Pound calls "the 'natural course of events' the exalted moment, the vision unsought or at least the vision gained without machination" (*Spirit of Romance* 97). In *The Spirit of Japanese Poetry* and *The Spirit of Romance*, Noguchi and Pound, respectively, emphasized this revelatory moment when high poetry must be written. But such a parallel in their poetics does not necessitate that one's ideas came from the other's. Pound's observations might have been made independently.

It is quite possible that Pound became acquainted through other sources with many of the superpository *hokku* that Noguchi cited as examples in *The Spirit of Japanese Poetry*. In addition to Moritake's "I Thought I Saw the Fallen Leaves" and Basho's "The Old Pond," quoted earlier, Noguchi translated the following: Buson's "Oh, How Cool—" (47) and "Prince Young, Gallant" (36), Basho's "Lying Ill on Journey" (38), and Hokushi's "It Has Burned Down" (27). It may be significant, however, that in another collection of critical essays Noguchi cited several of his own numerous *hokku* in English along with those by old masters. Many of Noguchi's English *hokku*, moreover, had been published in *The Pilgrimage* (1908, 1909). Pound might have acquainted himself with Noguchi's published *hokku* before he experimented with his version.

As Pound accounted for the circumstances of his metro poem in Paris in 1912, Noguchi also narrated the experience he had had in London in 1903:

> I myself was a *hokku* student since I was fifteen or sixteen years old; during many years of my Western life, now amid the California forest, then by the skyscrapers of New York, again in the London bus, I often tried to translate the *hokku* of our old masters but I gave up my hope when I had written the following in English:

> My Love's lengthened hair
> Swings o'er me from Heaven's gate:
> Lo, Evening's shadow!

> (Noguchi)

> It was in London, to say more particularly, Hyde Park, that I wrote the above *hokku* in English, where I walked slowly, my mind being filled with the thought of the long hair of Rossetti's woman as I perhaps had visited Tate's Gallery that afternoon. . . . I exclaimed then: "What use to try the impossibility in translation, when I have a moment to feel a *hokku* feeling and write about it in English?"[21]

Structurally, Pound's metro poem resembles Noguchi's Hyde Park *hokku*. As in Pound's poem where the outward image of the faces in the crowd is set on top of the inward image of petals on a wet, black bough, so the actual vision of an evening shadow in Noguchi's poem is juxtaposed to an envisioning of a woman's long hair. In each poem a pair of images, similar in form but different in content, coalesces into another autonomous image, which generates different meaning. The superposition of the paired images transforms into a different image in form and content, what Pound calls "the 'one image' poem" ("Vorticism" 467). This transformation of images retains the sensation of each separate object perceived, but it also conveys a greater sensation by uniting the two experiences.[22] For both poets, such a transformation is optimal, for they believe that images in poetry cannot and should not be divided as external and internal, physical and mental, objective and subjective.[23]

To illustrate the energy latent in this transformation of images, Pound provided an anecdote: "I once saw a small child go to an electric light switch and say, 'Mamma, can I open the light?' She was using the age-old language of exploration, the language of art" ("Vorticism" 466). Although he later became interested in Fenollosa's explanation that written Chinese characters denote action, he was first attracted to the poetics of the *hokku*, what he called "the sense of exploration . . . the beauty of this sort of knowing" ("Vorticism" 466–67). Noguchi expounded this poetics in terms of an intensive art by referring to Kikaku's celebrated *hokku*, as discussed earlier:

Autumn's full moon:
Lo, the shadows of a pine tree
Upon the mats!

(Kikaku, Noguchi, "What Is a Hokku Poem?" 357)

The beauty of the harvest moon is not only humanized but intensified by the shadow of a tree Kikaku saw on the *tatami* mats. "Really," Noguchi wrote, "it was my first opportunity to observe the full beauty of the light and shadow, more the beauty of the shadow in fact, far more luminous than the light itself, with such a decorativeness, particularly when it stamped the dustless mats as a dragon-shaped ageless pine tree" ("What Is a Hokku Poem?" 357). The situation here, shared by Pound and Noguchi, is one of finding, discovering, and hence inventing the new.

As if to bear out Pound's vorticist thinking in poetry, Noguchi made a modest proposal for English poets. "I think," he wrote, "it is time for them to live more of the passive side of Life and Nature, so as to make the meaning of the whole of them perfect and clear." To the Japanese mind, an intensive art can be created not from action, but from inaction. Noguchi thus argued that the larger part of life "is builded upon the unreality by the strength of which the reality becomes intensified" (*Spirit of Japanese Poetry* 24–25). Noguchi's paradox was echoed in Pound's statement about vorticism. To Pound, an intensive art is not an emphatic art. By an intensive art, Pound meant that "one is concerned with the relative intensity, or relative significance, of different sorts of expression. . . . They are more dynamic. I do not mean they are more emphatic, or that they are yelled louder" ("Vorticism" 468).

Pound illustrated this intensive art with a *hokku*-like sentence in his essay "Affirmations," first published in the *New Age* in 1915:

The pine-tree in mist upon the far hill looks
like a fragment of Japanese armour.

(Pound, "Vorticism" 468)

The images appear in simile form, but Pound has no intention of intensifying the beauty of either image by comparing it to that of the other. "In either case," he points out, "the beauty, in so far as it is beauty of form, is the result of 'planes in relation.' . . . The tree and the armour are beautiful because their diverse planes overlie in a certain manner." Unlike the sculptor or the painter, the poet, who must use words to intensify his art, Pound says, "may cast on the reader's mind a more vivid image of either the armour or the pine by mentioning them close together . . . for he works not with planes or with colours but with the names of objects and of properties. It is his business so to use, so to arrange, these names as to cast a more definite image than the layman can cast" (*Gaudier-Brzeska* 120–21).

Critics have shown over the years that Pound's idea of vorticism underlies not only his short imagistic poems, but also his longer pieces such as the *Cantos*, *Cathay*, and his translation of *noh* plays. Noguchi, on the other hand, attempted to intensify an image in a poem longer than the *hokku* by endowing it with action and autonomy. "The Passing of Summer" (1909), for instance, reads,

An empty cup whence the light of passion is drunk!—
To-day a sad rumour passes through the trees,
A chill wind is borne by the stream,
The waves shiver in pain;
Where now the cicada's song long and hot?

(Noguchi, Pilgrimage 1: 68)

Such visual images as an empty cup, the chilly wind blowing over the stream, and the shivering waves do not simply denote the passing of summer; they constitute its action. Similarly, experiences or memories of experiences like drinking "the light of passion" and hearing "the cicada's song long and hot" do not merely express the poet's nostalgia or sentiment about the summer; these images, rather than being metonymies, recreate the actions of the summer itself.[24] In Noguchi's poetry, as in the *hokku*, poetry and sensation are spontaneously conjoined and intensified, to leave no room for rationalism or moralism.

* * *

Numerous parallels between Pound's poetics and Noguchi's do not entail the conclusion that both poets held the same principles throughout their respective careers. Much of Noguchi's art and literary criticism shows great enthusiasm at times for Yeats's mysticism and Whitman's transcendentalism.[25] Noguchi had a taste for certain styles of poetry that Pound obviously did not. But what their writings as a whole suggest is that both writers, as poets and critics, agreed on the ideas of imagism during the period between 1908, when *The Pilgrimage*, Noguchi's fifth collection of English poems, appeared in Tokyo and London, and 1914, when Noguchi's *The Spirit of Japanese Poetry* was published in London. For Noguchi, this period came in the middle of his career as it coincided with Pound's early career and interest in imagism. This agreement on imagism constituted an interpenetrating relationship of Japanese poetics and Western intentions in early modernism. Pound's launching of Imagism in London in 1912 and 1913 with the support of T. E. Hulme, F. S. Flint, H. D., Richard Aldington, and others has become a legend of sorts. And much of the imagist work by various hands began to appear in Chicago in *Poetry* and in London in *Des Imagistes* and *The Freewoman* (later *The Egoist*). But the sources that Noguchi brought to Western attention as early as 1903, when *From the Eastern Sea*, the third collection of his English poems, was published in London, have become not only obscure but neglected.

In March 1913, Pound and his associates collectively drew up and published the three principles of their "faith." The first was "direct treatment of the 'thing,' whether subjective or objective." Noguchi would wholeheartedly have endorsed the formulation. The second principle called for "using absolutely no word that does not contribute to the presentation," and Noguchi had documented the practice of this tenet in the *hokku* by Japanese masters as well as in his own work. The third principle was "to compose in sequence of the musical phrase, not in sequence of the metronome" ("Vorticism" 462). Because the Japanese language radically differs from a Western language in rhythm, rhyme, stress, or tone, Noguchi would readily have assented to the proposal.

Much of Pound's early work and Noguchi's clearly reflects this accord between the imagists and Noguchi. It is true that while Pound was fascinated by haiku, he was also interested in vorticism as applied to visual arts, as his commentary on such artists as Gaudier-Brzeska, Brancusi, and Picasso indicates. Through the Poets' Club, Pound was also closely associated with Hulme, Flint, Aldington, Upward, and others, some of whom were initially attracted to Japanese color prints by such painters as Utamaro and Hokusai exhibited in the British Museum. There is clear evidence that Pound's associates also tried their hand at haiku with various degrees of seriousness and success. By the mid-1910s, imagism had indeed become the literary zeitgeist, and any poet living in London would have received some influence from the Japanese sources.

To sum up, then, Noguchi's English poems had been widely circulated in London well before September 1914, when Pound's vorticism essay appeared, and Noguchi's essay on *hokku* in *Rhythm* and his book *The Spirit of Japanese Poetry* were published in January 1913 and March 1914, respectively. The material in the essay and the book was delivered as a series of lectures during his stay in England from December 1913 to April 1914. In these circumstances, it is hardly conceivable that the imagists did not acquaint themselves with Noguchi's ideas. Even though Pound's modernist theory might partly have derived from other sources, one can scarcely overlook the direct link between haiku and Pound's imagism through Noguchi.

NOTES

1. See Earl Miner, "Pound, *Haiku* and the Image," *Hudson Review* 9 (Winter 1957): 570–84; and *Japanese Tradition*. There is some ambiguity in Miner's chronology since, in his article, the date of Pound's joining the Poets' Club is said to be "just before the first World War," which means perhaps between 1913 and 1914 ("Pound" 572). There is also another ambiguity with respect to the time and circumstance of Pound's learning about "the usefulness of Japanese poetry from Flint." Flint's interest in Japanese poetry is indicated in his own account of the matter, published in *The Egoist* for May 1, 1915: "I had been advocating in the course of a series of articles on recent books of verse a poetry in *vers libre*, akin in spirit to the Japanese" (*Japanese Tradition* 100).

2. For Noguchi's life and work, see Hakutani, ed. *Selected English Writings of Yone Noguchi: An East-West Literary Assimilation*, vol. 1: Poetry (1990) and vol. 2: Prose (1992). For a study of Noguchi's life, including an interview with his son, the late American sculptor Isamu Noguchi, see Hakutani, "Father and Son: A Conversation with Isamu Noguchi." For a discussion of Noguchi's English poetry and literary criticism, see Yoshinobu Hakutani, "Yone Noguchi's Poetry: From Whitman to Zen," *Comparative Literature Studies* 22 (1985): 67–79.

3. The impact of *hokku* on Pound was apparently greater and more beneficial than that on his fellow imagists. Regarding the form of superposition as ideal for expressing instantaneous perception, Pound wrote in a footnote, "Mr. Flint and Mr. Rodker have made longer poems depending on a similar presentation of matter. So also have Richard Aldington, in his *In Via Sestina*, and 'H. D.' in her *Oread*, which latter poems express much stronger emotions than that in my lines here given" ("Vorticism" 467). Pound's argument here suggests that *hokku* and Pound's *hokku*-like poems can express instantaneous and spontaneous perception better than can the longer poems and the poems with stronger emotions.

4. See Noguchi, "What Is a Hokku Poem?" *Rhythm* 11, no. 10 (January 1913): 354–59. The essay was reprinted in Noguchi's *Through the Torii* 126–39. The page numbers cited hereafter refer to the *Rhythm* version.

5. In a letter of November 24, 1913, to Pound, Mary Fenollosa wrote, "I am beginning with [*sic*] right now, to send you material." On the following day she wrote again, "Please don't get discouraged at the ragged way this manuscript is coming to you. As I said yesterday, it will all get there in time,—which is the most important thing." See Kodama, ed. *Ezra Pound and Japan: Letters and Essays* (Redding Ridge, CT: Black Swan Books, 1987), 6.

6. One of Pound's critics who acknowledge this fact, Roy E. Teele, demonstrates Fenollosa's failure to understand the Japanese language, particularly the essential rhythm of the *noh* text Fenollosa translated. See Teele, "The Japanese Translations," *Texas Quarterly* 10 (1967): 61–66.

7. Earl Miner, who states that Pound knew nothing about Japanese poetry before 1913 or 1914, believes that Pound later learned about *hokku* in the writings of the French translators ("Pound" 572–73).

8. See Noguchi, "The Everlasting Sorrow: A Japanese Noh Play," *Egoist* 4 (October 1917): 141–43, and "The Japanese Noh Play," *Egoist* 5 (August 1918): 99.

9. Noguchi first met Yeats in 1903 as indicated in a letter Noguchi wrote to Leonie Gilmour, his first wife: "I made many a nice young, lovely, kind friend among literary *genius* (attention!) W. B. Yeats or Laurence Binyon, Moore and Bridges. They are so good; they invite me almost every day" (Noguchi, *English Letters* 106). In 1921 Yeats, who was in Oxford, England, sent a long letter to Noguchi, who was in Japan, and wrote, in part, in reference to art and poetry: "The old French poets were simple as the modern are not, & I find in Francois Villon the same thoughts, with more intellectual power, that I find in the Gaelic poet [Raftery]. I would be simple myself but I do not know how. I am always turning over pages like those you have sent me, hoping that in my old age I may discover how. . . . A form of beauty scarcely lasts a generation with us, but it lasts with you for centuries. You no more want to change it than a pious man wants to change the Lord's Prayer, or the Crucifix on the wall [blurred] at least not unless we have infected you with our egotism" (Noguchi, *English Letters* 220–21).

10. See William Pratt, *Imagist Poem* (New York: Dutton, 1963), 14–15; J. B. Harmer, *Victory in Limbo: Imagism 1908–1917* (New York: St. Martin's, 1975), 17; Humphrey Carpenter, *Serious Character: The Life of Ezra Pound* (Boston: Houghton Mifflin, 1988), 115.

11. It is speculative, of course, but quite possible that Aldington, fascinated by Japanese visual arts, might have read the three articles about the subject Noguchi published in this period: "Utamaro," *Rhythm* 11, no. 10 (November 1912), 257–60; "Koyetsu," *Rhythm* 11, no. 11 (December 1912), 302–5; "The Last Master [Yoshitoshi] of the Ukiyoye School," *The Transactions of the Japan Society of London*, 12 (April 1914), 144–56. Moreover, *The Spirit of Japanese Art* (1915) includes chapters on major Japanese painters such as Koyetsu, Kenzan, Kyosai, and Busho Hara, besides Utamaro and Hiroshige. If Aldington had read these essays, he would very well have been acquainted with Noguchi's writings about Japanese poetics.

12. Aldington's poem reads:

The apparition of these poems in a crowd:
White faces in a black dead faint.

See Aldington, "Penultimate Poetry," *Egoist* (January 15, 1915). This poem sounds more like *senryu*, a humorous haiku, than the *hokku* Pound was advocating. *Senryu* originated from Karai Senryu, an eighteenth-century Japanese haiku poet.

13. See Davie, *Ezra Pound* 42 and Carpenter 247.

14. See Toyama, ed., *Essays on Yone Noguchi* (mostly in Japanese) 1: 327. Toyama, an art historian, was married to Yone Noguchi's daughter Hifumi.

15. See Jones, *Life and Opinions of Hulme* 122. Neither Noel Stock in *Poet in Exile: Ezra Pound* nor Humphrey Carpenter in *Serious Character* mentions Pound's activities at the Quest Society, let alone Pound's possible interactions with Noguchi.

16. See T. S. Eliot's introduction to *Literary Essays of Ezra Pound* 23.

17. About this time Noguchi also wrote an essay titled "A Japanese Note on Yeats," included in his book of essays, *Through the Torii* 110–17.

18. Noguchi's "Tell Me the Street to Heaven" was first published in his essay, "What Is a Hokku Poem?" *Rhythm* 11 (January 1913), 358, as indicated earlier, and

reprinted in *Through the Torii* (1914 and 1922). The other *hokku*, "Is It, Oh, List" was also included in the same issue and reprinted in *Through the Torii* with a change in the third line: "So runs Thames, so runs my Life" (136).

19. The original in Japanese reads *"Hiya-hiya to / Kabe wo fumaete / Hiru-ne kana."* See Henderson 49. The English translation of this haiku is by Hakutani.

20. Alan Durant tries to show that Pound's metro poem linguistically contains a number of metaphors and associations, and that it is not as imagistic as critics say. While Durant's interpretation is valid as far as the various elements in the poem appear to the reader as metaphors and associations, Pound's intention does differ from the reader's interpretation. The same thing may occur in the interpretation of a Japanese *hokku*, but traditionally the language of the *hokku*, as Noguchi demonstrates throughout *The Spirit of Japanese Poetry*, shuns metaphor and symbolism. See Alan Durant, "Pound, Modernism and Literary Criticism: A Reply to Donald Davie."

21. This passage is quoted from "Again on *Hokku*," included in *Through the Torii* 140–46. A *verbatim* account is given in the introduction to his *Japanese Hokkus* 22–23. For Noguchi's London experiences, see "My First London Experience (1903)" and "Again in London (1913–14)" in *Story of Yone Noguchi* 119–65.

22. The union of different experiences is reminiscent of T. S. Eliot's statement about an amalgamation. In reference to John Donne's poetry, Eliot writes: "When a poet's mind is perfectly equipped for its work, it is constantly amalgamating disparate experience; the ordinary man's experience is chaotic, irregular, fragmentary. The latter falls in love, or reads Spinoza, and these two experiences have nothing to do with each other, or with the noise of the typewriter or the smell of cooking; in the mind of the poet these experiences are always forming new wholes" (*Selected Essays* 247).

23. In *The Spirit of Japanese Poetry* Noguchi wrote: "As the so-called literary expression is a secondary matter in the realm of poetry, there is no strict boundary between the domains generally called subjective and objective; while some *Hokku* poems appear to be objective, those poems are again by turns quite subjective through the great virtue of the writers having the fullest identification with the matter written on. You might call such collation poetical trespassing; but it is the very point whence the Japanese poetry gains unusual freedom; that freedom makes us join at once with the soul of Nature" (43–44).

24. To the Japanese, such expressions as "the light of passion" and "the cicada's song" immediately evoke images of hot summer. These phrases in Japanese are attributed to or closely associated with summer.

25. For Whitman's influence on Noguchi, see Chapter 3 on Yone Noguchi.

Chapter 5

Haiku in English and Haiku Criticism in America

Among others in the West, Richard Wright (1908–1960) distinguished himself as a haiku poet by writing over 4,000 haiku in his last eighteen months of his life while in exile in Paris. When Wright turned to writing haiku he was certainly not working in an artistic vacuum. Artists in the Western world had been interested in haiku, its history and meaning, and had been writing haiku since early in the twentieth century. As a result of visits to Japan, French writers Julien Vocance, Paul-Louis Couchoud, and others began to write haiku in French. In 1910 a translation of a Japanese anthology of literature was made by Michael Revon, who referred to Basho's hokku as "haikai." Then in 1915 Vocance wrote a group of poems called *Cent Visions de Guerre* in the haiku form. By 1920 at least a dozen poets were writing haiku for the *Nouvelle revue française*. In London at the end of 1910, Basil Hall Chamberlain's second edition of Japanese poetry was published, with his essay "Basho and the Japanese Poetical Epigram."[1]

Soon American poets began to write haiku. The most famous was Ezra Pound, who wrote "In a Station of the Metro" in 1914. Some might consider this poem to be the first published haiku written in English in the West. Other Americans rapidly followed Pound's lead: Wallace Stevens in 1917, William Carlos Williams in 1919, and Amy Lowell in the same year. As early as 1909 the Imagist group of poets were influenced by both the *tanka* (a short verse form of live lines with 5, 7, 5, 7, 7 syllables respectively) and the haiku forms. The group included Ezra Pound, Amy Lowell, and John Gould Fletcher.[2] In 1915 in Boston, Lafcadio Hearn's translations of hokku and tanka were collected and published as *Japanese Lyrics*.[3] By the mid-1930s, Georges Bonneau began to publish a series of books, with his translation into French, of

Japanese poetry, *Le Haiku*. English translations of Japanese haiku by Harold
G. Henderson came out in 1934 as *The Bamboo Broom*.

The World War II temporarily sidetracked the Western world's interest in
haiku. But after the war, British writers in Tokyo began to renew Western
interest in haiku. The most important of these writers were Harold G. Henderson and R. H. Blyth. Their interest in haiku and subsequent books and translations once again made haiku a viable literary art form for Western poets.
Blyth showed with numerous classic haiku that the Buddhist ontologies and
Zen philosophy, in particular, underlie haiku composition. His *Haiku: Volume I*, the first of the four volumes, came out in 1949 and later was reissued
in 1952 under the title *Haiku*.

John Gould Fletcher introduced the West to Kenneth Yasuda's *A Pepper-
Pod*, a translation of Japanese haiku with selections of original haiku written
in English in 1946. Gary Snyder wrote haiku in his diary, published in 1952
under the title *Earth House Hold*. Allen Ginsberg read Blyth's work on haiku
and started to write haiku himself. An entry in his journal reads as follows:
"Haiku composed in the backyard cottage at . . . Berkeley 1955, while reading R. H. Blyth's 4 volumes *Haiku*." In 1958 Harold G. Henderson's revised
1930 work, retitled *An Introduction to Haiku*, appeared in America and
generated more interest in haiku. Another influential work that year was Jack
Kerouac's *The Dharma Bums*. Kerouac's character Japhy Ryder writes haiku
and had read a four-volume work on Japanese haiku. This was a reference to
Blyth's four volumes on haiku. In fact, numerous English speakers—American, Canadian, British, and others—began to write haiku.[4]

Harold G. Henderson, in *An Introduction to Haiku*, gives thanks to R.
H. Blyth, with whom he had had personal contact, and refers to Blyth's
"monumental four-volume work on haiku."[5] And William J. Higginson, in
The Haiku Handbook, refers to the American writer Richard Wright and says
that he had studied R. H. Blyth's books and "wrote several hundred [it was
actually more than four thousand] haiku during the last year and a half of his
life."[6]

Sometime during the summer of 1959 Wright had been introduced to haiku
by a young South African friend who loved its form.[7] Wright borrowed from
him Blyth's book, which discusses the art of haiku and the relationship of
haiku to Zen, and settled down to rediscover his old dream of oneness with
all life. By March 1960 he was so captivated by its beauty that he was already
in the midst of composing what was to turn out to be over four thousand
separate haiku. In response to a letter from his friend and Dutch translator,
Margrit de Sablonière, he said that he had returned to poetry and added,
"During my illness I experimented with the Japanese form of poetry called
haiku; I wrote some 4,000 of them and am now sifting them out to see if they
are any good."[8]

In his discussion of this event, Michel Fabre notes that Wright's interest in haiku involved his research into the great Japanese masters, Buson, Basho, and Issa. Wright ignored the European and American forms that were then becoming popular. Fabre notes further that Wright made "an effort to respect the exact form of the poem," and adds that it was curious for Wright to become interested in haiku at a time when he was fighting his illness. As Fabre reasons, "Logically he should have been tempted to turn away from 'pure' literature and to use his pen instead as a weapon."[9] Just as curiously, Wright's biographer Constance Webb refers to none of this material. She merely says that Wright had lost his physical energy and that "while lying against the pillows one afternoon he picked up the small book of Japanese poetry and began to read it again." Apparently it had been given to him earlier, and he read and reread it, excited by its style. She comments that Wright "had to study it and study to find out why it struck his ear with such a modern note." Then she adds that Wright "would try to bring the life and consciousness of a black American" to its form. Again according to Webb, the haiku "seemed to answer the rawness he felt, which had, in turn, created a sensitivity that ached. Never had he been so sensitive, as if his nervous system had been exposed to rough air" (Fabre, *Unfinished Quest* 505–6). In a letter to Paul Reynolds, his friend and editor, Wright said that he had sent to William Targ of the World Publishing Company a manuscript of his haiku.[10] In that same letter he commented that "these poems are the results of my being in bed a great A deal"[11] Until we read the poems in *Haiku: This Other World* and his 3,183 unpublished haiku we will probably never know the other reasons why Wright turned to haiku during the last years of his life.[12] But that knowledge, while helpful, is not necessary to reread and enjoy these newly published haiku. What is necessary, both for enjoyment and understanding of Wright's haiku, is some knowledge about haiku as the great Japanese poets developed the genre.

Back in 1955 Wright attended the Bandung Conference of the Third World; two years later he was a member of the First Congress of Negro Artists and Writers, which met in Paris in September. During that same period he liked to work in his garden on his Normandy farm, an activity that supplied many themes for his haiku. Of his experience in this period, Wright's travel to the newly independent Ghana in West Africa had a great impact on his writing of haiku. The African philosophy of life Wright witnessed among the Ashanti, "the African primal outlook upon life," as he called it, served as an inspiration for his poetic sensibility. Ezra Pound's theory that the poet's use of an image is not to support "some system of ethics or economics" coincides with a theory that haiku expresses the poet's intuitive worldview. Wright, then, found the haiku poet's intuitive worldview akin to that of the African.

***

Since 1998, when Wright's posthumous *Haiku: This Other World* was published, Wright's haiku have made an immediate impact on some of the contemporary American poets, most notably Robert Haas (1941–), Sonia Sanchez (1935–), James A. Emanuel (1921–), and Lenard D. Moore (1958–). Haas, U. S. Poet Laureate 1995–97, wrote in *The Washington Post*:

> Here's a surprise, a book of haiku written in his last years by the fierce and original American novelist Richard Wright. Wright changed American literature by writing books—"Native Son," "Black Boy"—about the fact that poverty, discrimination and hopelessness are not necessarily a formula for producing virtuous citizens. He wrote (especially in "Native Son," the novel that brought him to public attention and became an unexpected bestseller in 1940) about the consequences of racism with an angry exactness that took readers—black and white—by surprise. . . . What an outpouring! Wright's way with the form was to keep strictly to the syllable count of the Japanese tradition—five syllables, seven syllables, five syllables. ("Five Haikus by Richard Wright," *Washington Post*, April 11, 1999)

Not only was Haas deeply impressed by Wright's haiku, but his commentary on them also reveals how Wright had learned the theory and practice of haiku composition and applied them to the subtexts of his haiku, whether they were the French countryside, the rural Mississippi of his childhood, or the urban environments in Chicago, New York, Paris, and other cities. Among other subtexts, Haas considered "the pulse of his own life" the most original. He chose five haiku for his comments:

The first poem in the book suggests why the form was so useful to him:

I am nobody:
A red sinking autumn sun
Took my name away.

It lifted away from him for a moment his writer's vita, his radical's dossier, the fury of a life of literary controversy, and gave him permission to be, to look:

I give permission
For this slow spring rain to soak
The violet beds.

Many of the poems seem to be about paying attention, what the haiku form is so much about:

With a twitching nose
A dog reads a telegram

On a wet tree trunk.

Some of them look back on his own life and also seem to absorb into him his own mortality:

Burning autumn leaves,
I yearn to make the bonfire
Bigger and bigger.

That poem must be about aging, but it also has to pun on the angry black man Bigger Thomas, the protagonist of "Native Son." Enough commentary. Here is one more:

A sleepless spring night:
Yearning for what I never had
And for what never was.

("Five Haikus")

Among the initial reviews *Haiku: This Other World* received, one by William J. Higginson, author of *The Haiku Handbook* (1985), was most thorough and discerning. While Higginson considers some of Wright's haiku mediocre, he reads many of them as excellent haiku. To Higginson, not only was this edition the largest collection of haiku written in English, but it was the best haiku collection to come out of the 1950s and 1960s. Higginson, a haiku critic deeply impressed by Wright's works of prose, such as *Native Son* and *Black Boy*, is as deeply impressed by his haiku. In this review he points out that Wright's early poems focused mainly on the social and political environments and that his poetry turned out to be merely timely poems of protest. "Once his fiction and other prose writings made him famous," Higginson remarks, "his involvement with poetry diminished—until the last 18 months of his life" (*Santa Fe News*, February 21, 1999).

Higginson also points out, as noted earlier, that Wright acquired the theory and technique of haiku composition from R. H. Blyth, as did the writers of the Beats generation, such as Gary Snyder, Allen Ginsberg, and Jack Kerouac. Higginson also notes that Wright adhered to the traditional Japanese syllabic measure of 5–7–5, as well as to the requirement of *kigo* (seasonal reference) in many of his haiku.

With respect to the content and style of Wright's haiku, Higginson's comments on several of his favorite haiku by Wright are insightful. His reading and impression of these haiku is based on Wright's subtexts:

A somber tone pervades much of Wright's Haiku; he was ill while writing these haiku, and some of his closest friends and his mother died during this same period. Nonetheless, the collection shows a wider range of subject and tone than any other body of haiku in English from the period—a range fully justified by the range of Japanese haiku. The best poems among Wright's haiku exhibit the pure, significant observation, the delicate sensitivity, or the mysterious narrative fragment that characterize many of the best Japanese haiku, from an American perspective. Here are a few of my personal favorites:

The sound of the rain,
Blotted out now and then
By a sticky cough

The first day of spring:
A servant's hips shake as she
Wipes a mirror clean.

Standing in the field,
I hear the whispering of
Snowflake to snowflake.

(*Santa Fe News*, February 21, 1999)

Higginson is critical of some of Wright's haiku that "fall flat" because they sound like reports on social events. Wright is a master haiku poet, as Higgins shows, when his haiku reflect "the human comedy or give us a peek at an apparent mystery" (*Santa Fe News*). Higginson quotes these haiku as examples:

He hesitated
Before hanging up his coat
On the scarecrow's arm.

One autumn evening
A stranger enters a village
And passes on through.

In my sleep at night,
I keep pounding an anvil
Heard during the day.

This last is one of the very few poems in Wright's haiku that does not contain a seasonal reference, an element thought essential by most Japanese haiku poets. And this is one contribution the book makes, for American poets from the first have only somewhat paid lip-service to the seasons in their attempts at haiku; many ignore the seasons altogether. Some of Wright's haiku echo themes and even the language of poems found in Blyth's volumes. Here are two, with what may have been their unconscious models in Blyth's translations.

The sound of a rat
Scampering over cold tin
Is heard in the bowels.

The sound
Of a rat on a plate,-
How cold it is! (Buson)

A shaggy brown dog
Squatting under winter trees,
Shitting in the rain.

A stray cat
Excreting
In the winter garden. (Shiki)

Of Shiki's poem, Blyth says "This is an extraordinarily good haiku." Wright's language is as direct as Shiki's, which Blyth's is not. There are many poems of stark, harsh reality in Wright's collection, and many more that simply don't make the grade. But, poem for poem, Wright's haiku is the best large American haiku collection . . . and the only full collection of haiku by a major American writer to remotely suggest both the range and depth possible in the genre. (*Santa Fe News*)

Leza Lewitz, another reviewer, wrote, "*Haiku: This Other World* is an outstanding addition to Wright's literary and humanist achievements and stands as a beacon to this other world, masterful and free" (*Japan Times*, April 27, 1999). She found the nexus between Wright's haiku and the illness Wright was battling in his last years in Paris. "As his illness worsened," Lewitz observes,

Wright reflected on another world beyond race or politics—this other world just beneath the surface of everyday perception—and magnified its moments with humor, joy, dignity and a kind of imagistic delicacy, while touching on those broader themes. And where his writing was once forceful and direct, here it is gentle and suggestive:

In the falling snow
A laughing boy holds out his palms
Until they are white.

While nature plays a large role in Wright's haiku, and humor can be found in the many "senryu" collected here, the themes of loss, betrayal, exile, wandering, mourning and longing surface over and over again. Yet, haiku seems to have offered Wright a kind of nurturing in the face of his own death, a spiritual home in exile. It's almost as if by accepting the cyclical spirit of nature rather than struggling against it, one can accept the human spirit with all of its inherent contradictions and losses. Ultimately, one finds a kind of home. (*Japan Times*, April 27, 1999)

Lewitz's reading of some of Wright's haiku as reflections of his illness echoes that of Julia Wright. Julia Wright, "an immature eighteen-year-old" as she called herself, was gravely concerned about her father's deteriorating health as she watched her father hang, on metal rods in his narrow studio, hundreds of sheets on which the haiku were typed. She read this haiku at his memorial service:

Burning out its time,
And timing its own burning,
One lonely candle.

Lewitz also remarks that many of Wright's haiku reflects his thoughts about human mortality. In 1958 Edward Aswell, his trusted editor and friend, died, and a year later another close friend, George Padmore, with whom Wright was planning another travel to Africa, also died. In the same year Wright was deeply shocked as he heard Camus, whom he had admired, was killed in a car accident. Julia Wright was also a witness to her father's long mourning over his mother's death. These haiku are, she felt, "Wright's poetry of loss and retrieval, of temperate joy and wistful humor, of exile and fragments of a dreamed return" ("Introduction" to *Haiku: This Other World* xii).

***

The publication of Wright's haiku, some of which appeared in 1978, has inspired several American poets to write haiku, not to mention numerous haiku enthusiasts in the English speaking world. Among them Sonia Sanchez (1934-) has published two collections of haiku: *Like the Singing Coming Off the Drums* (1998) and *Morning Haiku* (2010). While Sanchez is known as an activist poet, much of her poetic impulse *in Like the Singing Coming off the Drums* (1998) derives from the tradition of Japanese haiku, in which a poet pays the utmost attention to the beauty inherent in nature. A great majority of *Like the Singing Coming Off the Drums* are entitled haiku, *tanka*, or *sonku*. Reading such poems indicates that Sanchez, turning away from the moral, intellectual, social, and political problems dealt with in her other work, found in nature, as did Wright, her latent poetic sensibility. Above all, her fine pieces of poetry show, as do classic Japanese haiku and *tanka* (short song), the unity and harmony of all things, the sensibility that nature and humanity are one and inseparable. In this collection, much of her poetry poignantly expresses a desire to transcend social and racial differences and a need to find union and harmony with nature.

Both Sanchez and classic Japanese haiku poets are always inspired by the visual beauty in which nature presents itself. Buson was well known in his time as a professional painter as he is today, and many of his haiku reflect his singular attention to color and its intensification. One of Sanchez's haiku included in the middle section, "Shake Loose My Skin," and one of the longer poems entitled "A Poem for Ella Fitzgerald" both thrive on colorful imagery. The haiku reads:

i am you loving
my own shadow watching
this noontime butterfly.

(61)

"A Poem for Ella Fitzgerald," the longest poem in this collection, is focused on these lines:

the moon turned red in the sky,
[...............................]
nightingales in her throat
[...............................]
an apollo stage amid high-stepping
yellow legs
[...............................]

(104–5)

"Shake Loose My Skin" and "A Poem for Ella Fitzerald" are both reminiscent of Buson's "Also Stepping On," a haiku that can be compared to Wright's haiku "A butterfly makes / The sunshine even brighter / With fluttering wings" :

Also stepping on
The mountain pheasant's tail is
The spring setting sun.[13]

For a seasonal reference to spring, Buson links an image of the bird with spring sunset, because both are highly colorful. As a painter he is also fascinated by an ambiguous impression the scene he has drawn gives him; it is not clear whether the setting sun is treading on the pheasant's tail or the tail on the setting sun. In any event, Buson has made both pictures beautiful to behold. In Sanchez's haiku, "I Am You Loving," it is ambivalent whether the focus is on "my own shadow" or "this noontime butterfly"; both constitute beautiful images of nature. Likewise "A Poem for Ella Fitzgerald" juxtaposes the image of the red moon with that of nightingales. Sanchez in these poems creates, as does Buson in his, a pair of counter images, themselves highly colorful and bright, which in turn intensify each other.

The predilection to portray human life in close association with nature means that the poet is more interested in genuinely natural sentiments than in moral, ethical, or political problems. Looking at the wind as a primal signifier of nature, Sanchez composed two poems in "Naked in the Streets," one entitled "Haiku" and the other "Blues Haiku":

how fast is the wind
sailing? how fast did i go
to become slow?

(38)

let me be yo wil
derness let me be yo wind
blowing you all day.

(39)

Traditionally, another singular, awe-inspiring signifier of nature in haiku is silence. Besides "The Old Pond," Basho is also known for another haiku that concerns nature's silence, "How Quiet It Is," another well-known haiku that was earlier compared to Wright's haiku on a similar subject:

How quiet it is!
Piercing into the rocks
The cicada's voice.[14]

In the middle section "Shake Loose My Skin," Sanchez wrote this haiku:

how still the morning sea
how still this morning skin
anointing the day.

(50)

Just as Basho was awed by the silence pervading the backdrop of the scene in contrast to "the shrill of cicada," Sanchez is struck by the equation between the stillness of "the morning sea" and that of "this morning skin." Richard

Wright, perhaps influenced by Basho, composed the following pair of haiku in which he focused on nature's silence:

>   In the silent forest
> A woodpecker hammers at
>   The sound of silence.

(Wright, Haiku 79)

>   A thin waterfall
> Dribbles the whole autumn night,—
>   How lonely it is.[15]

(Wright, Haiku 143)

What is common in these haiku by the three poets is that the scene is drawn with little detail and the mood is provided by a simple, reserved description of fact. These haiku create the kind of beauty associated with the aesthetic sensibility of *sabi* that suggests loneliness and quietude as opposed to over-excitement and loudness.[16]

Traditionally as well, the haiku in its portrayal of human beings' association with nature expresses the poet's enlightenment, a new way of looking at humanity and nature. In some of her poems in *Like the Singing Coming off the Drums*, Sanchez follows this tradition. The second stanza in "Love Poem [*for Tupac*]," the following lines,

> the old ones
> [.............]
> just passing
> through into
> [.............]

(111)

suggests Sanchez's fascination with the Buddhist theory of transmigration. The Buddhist concept of reincarnation, as discussed in my reading of Wright's *Black Power*, has a striking affinity with the Akan concept of life and death. Buddhism and the Akan religion share the belief, as does Lacan, that death is not the opposite of life but that death is a continuation of life.[17]

The following haiku expresses not only the concept of reincarnation, but also an enlightenment in Zen philosophy:

> what is done is done
> what is not done is not done
> let it go . . . like the wind.

(27)

The last line "let it go . . . like the wind" spontaneously expresses the truth about nature and humanity. Some of Sanchez's haiku like this one have an affinity with the Zen concept of *mu*. This state of nothingness, as discussed earlier, is devoid of all thoughts and emotions that are derived from human subjectivity and egotism and contrary to the conscious or unconscious truth represented by nature. An enlightened person is liberated from the self-centered worldview, convention, or received opinion that often lacks fairness and justice. While Sanchez, in the first two lines of this haiku, describes facts in human life, she in the last line gives an admonition as a Zen master that one must emulate the principles of nature in molding one's conduct and action.

Not only do many of Sanchez's haiku follow Zen doctrine, they also share the aesthetic principles that underlie classic haiku. One of the most delicate principles of Eastern art is called "yugen," mentioned earlier. Originally *yugen* in Japanese art was an element of style pervasive in the language of *noh*. It was also a philosophical principle originated in Zen metaphysics. In Zen, every individual possesses Buddhahood and must realize it. *Yugen*, as applied to art, designates the mysterious and dark, what underlies the surface. The mode of expression, as noted earlier, is subtle as opposed to obvious, suggestive rather than declarative. *Yugen* functions in art as a means by which human beings can comprehend the course of nature. Although *yugen* seems allied with a sense of resignation, it has a far different effect upon the human psyche. The style of *yugen* can express either happiness or sorrow.

The sense of loss also underlies the principle of *yugen*. Sanchez's first *tanka* in "Naked in the Street" expresses such a sentiment:

i thought about you
the pain of not having
you cruising my bones.
[.........................]
[.........................]

(18)

A pair of blues haiku, included in the same section, figure a brightened sense of *yugen*:

when we say good-bye
i want yo tongue inside my
mouth dancing hello.

(16)

you too slippery
for me. can't hold you long or
hard. not enough nites.

(17)

As aesthetic principles, *yugen* and the blues share the sentiments derived from private and personal feelings. As modes of expression, the blues stylistically differs from *yugen* since, as Amiri Baraka has observed, the blues "issued directly out of the shout and of course the spiritual" (62). Whereas *yugen* is characterized by reservation and modesty, the blues tradition calls for a worldly excitement and love. Unlike *yugen*, the blues confine its attention solely to the immediate and celebrates the bodily expression: both "When We Say Good-Bye" and "You Too Slippery" convey direct, unreserved sexual manifestations. Most importantly, Sanchez tries to link the blues message with sexually charged language so as to liberate black bodies from the distorted images slavery inflicted.

That the blues tradition has a greater impact on Sanchez's poetry than does the aesthetics of *yugen* can be seen how Sanchez constructs her imagery. If imagery in classic haiku is regarded as indirect and suggestive, the imagery in Sanchez's poetry has the directness and clarity of good prose as opposed to the suggestiveness and vagueness of symbolist poetry. The first poem in "Naked in the Streets" has an extremely sensuous image: dancing is described in terms of "corpuscles sliding in blood" (3). In the second poem of the same section, a haiku quoted earlier, the central image of running "naked in the streets" does not suggest anything other than what it describes:

you ask me to run
naked in the streets with you
i am holding your pulse.

(4)

In another poem, a blues haiku, in "Shake Loose My Skin," a series of images consist of instantaneous actions:

legs wrapped around you
camera. action. tightshot.
this is not a rerun.

(68)

Both poems have an affinity with imagistic poems in the expression of love, such as Pound's "Alba," discussed earlier in Chapter 4 on Pound, imagism, and haiku.

As cool as the pale wet leaves
    of lily-of-the-valley
        She lay beside me in the dawn.

(*Personae* 109)

In this haiku-like poem what Pound expressed was not the personal feeling he had about the woman lying beside him at dawn but his spontaneous sensation of the coolness of "the pale wet leaves / of lily-of-the-valley." Likewise, the actions themselves of running "naked in the streets" and "legs wrapped around you" were Sanchez's subjects in the poems.

Such poems as "You Ask Me to Run" and "Legs Wrapped Around You" bear a structural resemblance as well to Pound's famous imagistic haiku, "In a Station of the Metro," quoted earlier. Unlike Sanchez's haiku, Pound's "In a Station of the Metro" is constructed in two lines simply because Pound had in mind "a form of super-position" in which the poem was to be composed. "In a poem of this sort," he explained, "one is trying to record the precise instant when a thing outward and objective transforms itself, or darts into a thing inward and subjective" ("Vorticism" 467). Compared to Pound's "In a Station of the Metro," Sanchez's "You Ask Me to Run" has a similar structure in imagery. Just as in the other haiku, "Legs Wrapped Around You," Sanchez in this poem is trying to record the precise instant when a thing outward and objective, that is, running "naked in the streets," transforms itself or darts into a thing inward and subjective, that is, the image of "i am holding your pulse." The image of running "naked in the streets" is based in immediate experience, whether real or imagined since Sanchez lived in Philadelphia. Not only did she see the "thing," it must have generated such a sensation that she could not shake it out of her mind.

Although most of the short poems collected in *Like the Singing Coming Off the Drums* are stylistically influenced by the poetics of haiku as well as by the aesthetics of modernist poetry, much of Sanchez's ideological concern is postmodern, postcolonial, and African American. Many of her poems aim at teaching African Americans to achieve individualism and value their heritage. Even such a haiku as

mixed with day and sun
i crouched in the earth carry
you like a dark river.

(36)

succinctly expresses what Langston Hughes does in "The Negro Speaks of Rivers":

I've known rivers:
I've known rivers ancient as the world and older than the flow of human
        blood in human veins.

My soul has grown deep like the rivers.

Hughes reminds readers of the ancient rivers such as the Euphrates, the Congo, and the Nile, and then lead them to the most important river for African Americans, the Mississippi:

I bathed in the Euphrates when dawns were young.
I built my hut near the Congo and it lulled me to sleep.
I looked upon the Nile and raised the pyramids above it.
I heard the singing of the Mississippi when Abe Lincoln went down to New
    Orleans, and I've seen its muddy bosom turn all golden in the sunset.

(Selected Poems 4)

Sanchez and Hughes are both portraying how the African American soul, a symbol of humanity, is deeply embedded in the earth. The soul, as Hughes sees, "has grown deep like the rivers"; anyone endowed with it, like Sanchez, carries anyone else "like a dark river."

Hughes's signifying thrives on a chain of signs, signifiers, and signifieds. While "the Euphrates," "the Congo," "the Nile," and "the Mississippi" are all signs of great rivers, they also signify different human histories. All the signifieds in turn signify yet other historical events. For African Americans, "the Mississippi" signifies its "singing . . . when Abe Lincoln went down to New Orleans"; not only does it signify "its muddy bosom," but its signified in turn signifies a beautiful image, the golden river under sunset. Sanchez's haiku, on the other hand, is comprised of fewer but nonetheless equally powerful signs, signifiers, and signifieds: the words "mixed," "day," "sun," "i," "crouched," "earth," "carry," "you," "dark," and "river." These words express natural, spontaneous human sentiments, as do those in classic haiku, rather than emotional, personal feelings. In fact, an epiphany given in Sanchez's haiku, "Mixed with Day and Sun," bears a strong resemblance to a cross-cultural vision captured in Hughes's "The Negro Speaks of Rivers."

Sanchez' most important thematic concern is love of humanity, an act of faith that must begin with self-love. The last poem in the collection, dedicated to Gwendolyn Brooks, is a response and rejoinder to such a poem as Brooks's "The Mother." Not only is Brooks portrayed as "a holy one," she has become a universal symbol of the mother with enduring love and humanity:

For she is a holy one
[......................]
so that we live and
[......................]
breathe and love and

(133)

The sign that Sanchez's "For Sister Gwen Brooks" shares with Brooks's "The Mother" signifies the universal vision that love emanates from mother. Sanchez's refrain "for she is a holy one" further signifies the goddess worshiped among the Ashanti and the female king who owns her children, as described in Richard Wright's *Black Power*. In *Pagan Spain*, as Wright speculates, the universal motherhood has derived from the Virgin Mary, "Maya, the mother of Buddha," and "Isis, mother of Horus." As Wright remarks, "Egyptians worshiped Isis . . . and she was called Our Lady, the Queen of Heaven, Mother of God" (*Pagan Spain* 65).

The penultimate poem in *Like the Singing Coming off the Drums* is dedicated to Cornel West. In contrast to the rest of the poems it is a prose poem like Whitman's "Song of Myself." Cornel West, a Harvard professor, is not presented as a spokesman of the academia but characterized as a cultural activist like Whitman, Hughes, and Brooks, each of whom in a unique way sought to apotheosize the humanity of the land. Sanchez sees West as a foremost individual at the dawn of the twenty-first century, a spokesperson always examining a nation that denies the sanctity of the human rights. Sanchez urges the reader to take a serious look at this radical and yet eminently positive individual. West is

> This man . . . pulling us . . . towards a future that will hold all of humankind in an embrace . . . The poor. Blacks and whites. Asians and Native Americans. Jews and Muslims. Latinos and Africans. Gays and Lesbians (131).[18]

Rather than dwelling on the racial conflict and oppression the country has suffered, Sanchez admonishes the reader to see cross-pollination in the various cultures brought together to the land.

Whether *Like the Singing Coming off the Drums* is Sanchez's best work remains to be seen in the generations to come, but an effort to use diverse principles of aesthetics in molding her poetry has few precedents in American literature. Thematically, nineteenth-century American writers like Emerson, Poe, Dickinson, and Whitman were partly influenced by various cultural and religious thoughts as twentieth-century American writers like Ezra Pound, Wallace Stevens, Richard Wright, Allen Ginsberg, Jack Kerouac, and Gary Snyder at some points in their careers emulated Eastern poetics. Sanchez, on the other hand, remains one of the accomplished contemporary American poets writing from the perspective of cross-cultural visions for the form and content of her poetry.

***

The posthumous publication of Richard Wright's haiku inspired James Emanuel (1921–2013), an African American poet, to write haiku as it had an impact on Sonia Sanchez. Like Wright and Sanchez, Emanuel became frustrated with the state of racism in America. Like Wright, Emanuel went into exile in Europe and died in Paris. Like Wright, Emanuel wrote haiku in France. As Sanchez related the aesthetic of haiku with that of blues music, Emanuel found a strong affinity between haiku and jazz. With the publication of *Jazz from the Haiku King* (1999), he created a new literary genre, jazz haiku, often read with musical accompaniment throughout Europe and Africa.

Even on the surface there is much in common between jazz and haiku. As jazz performance thrives on an endless improvisation the composer makes out of traditional materials, so does haiku composition on an infinite improvisation upon beautiful objects in nature and humanity. Because of improvisation, the composer in both genres must efface his or her identity. In jazz, play changes on ideas as well as on sounds so as to create unexpected sensations. In haiku, the poet spares no pains to capture unexpected sensations. In both genres, the composer and the composed, subject and object, coalesce as the identity of the composer disappears in the wake of creation.

Jazz also shares many of the philosophical principles that underlie haiku. As noted earlier, haiku since Basho has traditionally been associated with Zen philosophy. Zen teaches the follower to attain enlightenment, a new way of looking at humanity and nature. Just as Zen stresses self-reliance, not egotism, and nature, not materialism, so does jazz. Like haiku, jazz, characterized by innovation, seeks a new way of looking at ourselves and the world around us. As jazz challenges us to hear the sounds and rhythms we have not heard before, so does haiku to see the images of humanity and nature we have not seen before. Jazz and haiku enable us to open our minds and imagine ways of reaching a higher ground in our present lives.

In contrast to the blues and the spirituals, jazz is well known for improvisation and syncopation. Individualism, which also distinguishes jazz, aside, another salient feature of jazz is the anonymity of jazz artists, as Ralph Ellison observes:

> Some of the most brilliant of jazzmen made no records; their names appeared in print only in announcements of some local dance or remote "battles of music" against equally uncelebrated bands. Being devoted to an art which traditionally thrives on improvisation, these unrecorded artists very often have their most original ideas enter the public domain almost as rapidly as they are conceived to be quickly absorbed into the thought and technique of their fellows. Thus the riffs which swung the dancers and the band on some transcendent evening, and which inspired others to competitive flights of invention, become all too swiftly a part of the general style, leaving the originator as anonymous as the creators of the architecture called Gothic. (*Shadow* 234)

The anonymity of jazz musicians has an affinity with that of *noh* dramatists. W. B. Yeats, inspired by *noh* drama, wrote such a play as *At the Hawk's Well.*

In the performance of the play, Yeats used masks to present anonymous, time-honored expressions as the Roman theater used the mask instead of make-ups (Noguchi, *Spirit of Japanese Poetry* 60). Yeats clearly implied in his letter to Yone Noguchi that contemporary arts in the West were infected with egotism while classical works of art in Japan were created as if anonymously (Noguchi, *Selected Writings* 2: 14).

What seemed to have inspired Yeats was the "simplicity" of the artists, an ancient form of beauty that transcends time, place, and personality. Irked by modern ingenuity and science, he was adamantly opposed to realism in art and literature. For him realism failed to uncover the deeply ingrained human spirit and character. He later discovered that noble spirits and profound emotions are expressed with simplicity in the *noh* play. Noguchi observed, "It was the time when nobody asked who wrote them, if the plays themselves were worthy. What a difference from this day of advertisement and personal ambition! . . . I mean that they are not the creation of one time or one age; it is not far wrong to say that they wrote themselves, as if flowers or trees rising from the rich soil of tradition and Buddhistic faith" (*Spirit of Japanese Poetry* 63). In its simplicity and appeal, jazz has much in common with *noh* drama.

Unlike the blues, jazz is characterized by its flexibility and creativity. As the blues emphasizes individuality and personality, jazz does anonymity and impersonality. While both individuality and communal affirmation are central to the blues, their relationship and importance to jazz are different from those to the blues. "Seen in relation to the blues impulse," Craig Werner observes, "the jazz impulse provides a way of exploring implications of realizing the relational possibilities of the (blues) self, and of expanding the consciousness of self and community through a process of continual improvisation" (*Playing* xxii). Involving both self expression and community affirmation, jazz is a genre of ambivalence and of what Ellison calls "a cruel contradiction." He remarks:

> For true jazz is an art of individual assertion within and against the group. Each true jazz moment (as distinct from the uninspired commercial performance) springs from a contest in which each artist challenges all the rest; each solo flight, or improvisation, represents (like the successive canvasses of a painter) a definition of his identity: as individual, as member of the collectivity and as a link in the chain of tradition. (*Shadow* 234)

In light of the relation of self and community, jazz also bears a strong resemblance to *renga*, the Japanese linked song, from which haiku evolved. *Renga*, which flourished in the beginnings as comic poetry was a continuous chain of fourteen (7–7) and seventeen (5–7–5) syllable verses, each independently composed, but connected as one poem, a communal composition.[19]

Jazz in the early 1950s, on the other hand, emphasized individuality, in technical virtuosity and theoretical knowledge, rather than community and its involvement with jazz. "In response," Werner notes, "jazz musicians such as Miles Davis, Ornett Coleman, and John Coltrane established the contours of the multifaceted 'free jazz' movement, which includes most AACM [the Association for the Advancement of Creative Musicians] work" (*Playing* 247). As Gayl Jones has also remarked, jazz, rendered through nonchronological syncopation and tempo, thrives on the essence of jazz, "the jam session," that "emerges from an interplay of voices improvising on the basic themes or motifs of the text in keywords and phrases." This interplay of self and other and self and community, what Jones calls "seemingly nonlogical and associational," makes the jazz text more complex, flexible, and fluid than the blues text (*Liberating* 200). Jazz, as Louis Armstong said, is a genre of music that should never be played in the same way as before.[20]

Jazz and haiku both convey spontaneously created expressions that are free from any economic, social, or political impulses. "Jazz," he writes in his preface, "I knew—like the Caruso I heard on the same phonograph—had no boundaries; but its immense international magnetism seemed inadequately explored in poetry" (iv-v). In haiku, despite its brevity, he found much of the height and depth of vision as he did in jazz.

In the haiku, "Dizzy's Bellows Pumps," under the title "Dizzy Gillespie (News of His Death,)" placed in the middle of the collection,

Dizzy's bellows pumps.
Jazz balloon inflates, floats high.
Earth listens, stands by.

(44)

Emanuel hears Gillespie's music reverberate in the sky and on earth. Traditionally haiku express and celebrate the unity of humanity and nature: a part of a haiku usually has a *kigo* (seasonal word). Even though Emanuel's "Dizzy's Bellows Pumps" lacks a seasonal reference, it displays the nexus of humanity and nature: Gillespie and sky and earth. This haiku is an elegy as Whitman's "When Lilacs Last in the Dooryard Bloom'd" is an elegy for Lincoln. In celebrating the lives of the great men, both poems express the immortality of their spirits. As Lincoln will return with lilacs in the spring and the northern star at night, Gillespie will be remembered for his jazz.

Emanuel's haiku on Gillespie is also remindful of Zen philosophy, which emphasizes the fusion of humanity and nature. Zen teaches its followers to transcend the dualism of life and death. Zen master Dogen observed that life and death are not separated as they seem and that there is no need to avoid death. Similarly, Emanuel and Whitman both seek a reconciliation of life and death. Whitman's feat of turning the national bereavement in the elegy into a celebration of death is well known, but less known is his idea of death given in "A Sight in Camp in the Daybreak Gray and Dim." To Whitman, the dead soldier in this poem appears no less divine than the savior Christ; they both represent the living godhead. In a similar vein, as Gillespie's jazz balloon floats high in the sky and the earth stands by and listens, this jazz master is vividly alive.

Emanuel captures the affinity of jazz and haiku in many of the poems in the collection. The first chapter "Page One" features various types of jazz haiku with translations into other languages: "The Haiku King," "Jazzanatomy," "Jazzroads," "Jazzactions," "Bojangles and Jo." The first of the four poems under the group title "Jazzanatomy" reads:

EVERYTHING is jazz:
snails, jails, rails, tails, males, females,
snow-white cotton bales.

(2)

To Emanuel, jazz represents all walks of life, human and nonhuman alike. Human life is represented by males and females, animal life by snails and tails, and inanimate life by snow-white. "My haiku," Emanuel remarks in his preface, "added the toughness of poverty and racial injustice" (iv). The images of "jails" and "cotton bales," signifying the unjustified imprisonment of African Americans and their immoral slave labor, represent the twin evils in American life: racism and poverty. In "Song of Myself," a narrative and autobiographical poem, also concerns all walks of American life. Focusing on human life, Whitman declares, "I am the poet of the Body and I am the poet of the Soul," and "I am the poet of the woman the same as the man." About the problems of good and evil, he writes, "The pleasures of heaven are with me and the pains of hell are with me" (*Complete Poetry* 39).

Emanuel's view of humanity and nature is shared by his American pre-decessors, such as Whitman, Countee Cullen, and Wright. The opening pages of Wright's *Black Power* has a passage addressed "To the Unknown African" and two quotations from Cullen and Whitman. "To the Unknown African" records an observation derived from Wright's view that the African was victimized by slave trades because of the African's primal outlook on human existence. The quotations from both Cullen and Whitman suggest that Africans, the inheritors and products of nature, have been exploited by a materialistic civilization. Before Europeans appeared with their machines, the continent had thrived on its pastoral idylls. Now it exists at the services of Western traders who exploit African products. Whitman's line *"Not till the sun excludes you do I exclude you,"* quoted in *Black Power*, expresses not merely his compassion for African Americans but strongly, as do Cullen's lines, their natural and divine heritage.[21]

From a philosophical perspective, Emanuel's jazz haiku have an affinity with the Zen concept of *mu*, as do many of Jack Kerouac's haiku. A series of ten haiku in the chapter "Jazz Meets the Abstract (Engravings)," for example, describe various human actions in which Emanuel is in search of space, a Zen-like state of nothingness. This space is devoid of egotism and artificiality: it transcends human reasoning and personal vision. In the first haiku,

Space moves, contours grow
as wood, web, damp, dust. Points turn,
Corners follow. JAZZ!

(87)

Jazz creates a space that moves as its contours "grow / as wood, web, damp, dust," their points "turn," and their corners "follow." Neither intellectuality nor emotion such as hatred and anger is able to occupy such a space.

Emanuel further shows, in his jazz haiku, the state of nothingness, which jazz is able to achieve:

No meaning at birth:
just screams, squirms, frowns without sight,
fists clenched against light.

(88)

Jazz is like a new born child with its "fists clenched against light." The child just "screams, squirms, frowns without sight": all this has "No meaning at birth," a state of nothingness. In the next pair of jazz haiku,

Abstract, I try you
(walk, sit, stretch). You say nothing.
Good fit; to wit: JAZZ.

(90)

No dust, rust, no guilt
in home JAZZ built; it cheers, STANDS,
charms guests from ALL lands.

(93)

Emanuel tries jazz, as he does an infant, "(walk, sit, stretch)." Like the infant, jazz says "nothing," *mu*, but is a good fit. Such a space has "No dust, rust," and such a state of mind has "no guilt." Whereas jazz was born and reared in America, it has attracted "guests from ALL lands." To Emanuel, jazz and

Zen, characteristic of their respective cultures, have a common, universal appeal.

In other jazz haiku, he also envisions the world in which the state of *mu* can be attained. In this haiku, for example,

Soars, leapfrogs, yells: JAZZ!
But don't expect no tantrums,
no crazyman spells.

(6)

height and intensity define jazz: it "Soars, leapfrogs, yells." Emanuel cautions, however, that soaring sounds and "yells" do not signal "tantrums" and "crazyman spells." The sound of jazz, like the sound of the water made by a leaping frog in Basho's haiku, signifies enlightenment, the state of *mu*. Just as Basho is impressed with the depth and silence of the universe, so is Emanuel with the height and intensity of jazz. This state of consciousness jazz creates has the effect of cleansing the human mind of impurity. The Haiku on Louis Armstrong,

Jazz-rainbow: skywash
his trumpet blew, cleansing air,
his wonderworld there.

(56)

captures Armstrong's ability to create his utopia, a "wonderworld," purified of social ills and racial conflicts.

Armstrong's utopia is, in turn, buttressed by individualism. The last four haiku under the title "Steppin' Out on the Promise" in chapter V, "Jazzmix," urge on African Americans the imperative of individualism. The first pair of jazz haiku addresses Brother and Sister:

Step out, Brother. Blow.
Just pretend you plantin' corn,
gold seeds from your horn.

Step out, Sister. Blow.
Must be Lord told you to play,
gifted you that way.

(84)

Emanuel impels each of the African Americans, brothers and sisters, sons and daughters, to be individualistic, self-reliant in their efforts to realize the Promised Land. He tells his brother to blow his horn and plant "gold seeds"

from it; he tells his sister to blow her horn and play the way God told her.
The second pair then addresses Daughter and Son:

Step out, Daughter. Shine.
Make 'em switch their lights on, chile.
Make 'em jazzophile.

Step out, Sonny. Blow.
Tell 'em all they need to know.
Lay it on 'em. GO!

(84)

Emanuel urges his daughter to shine in her performance and make her audience "jazzophile" as he tells his son to blow his horn and enlighten his audience with "all they need to know." Emanuel's command "Step out," which
begins each of the jazz haiku, emphasizes the principles of subjectivity and
individuality in jazz performance. Each of the jazz haiku above, unlike a classic haiku, is united in its rhythm and meaning by a rhyme between the last
two lines: "corn" and "horn," "play" and "way," "chile" and "jazzophile,"
"know " and "GO!"

Adding rhyme to haiku, much like deleting seasonal reference, is an innovation Emanuel has made in his haiku. He has attempted to widen the sensory
impact of haiku beyond the effect of the single impression given in a traditional haiku. Jazz is not only an expression of African American individualism, but it also inspires African Americans into cooperation and dialogue.
A series of haiku under the title "Jazz as Chopsticks" feature the unity and
cooperation of two individuals:

If Twin's the arrow,
Chops plays bow. No JAZZ fallin'
if they both don't go.

Chops makes drum sounds SPIN.
Twin coaxes them, herds them in,
JAZZ their next of kin.
[.................................]
When stuck on his lick,
Chops runs the scale. Twin slides loose,
then harpoons the whale.

"Chops, whatcha doin'?"
"Waitin' for Twin. It's my bass
his melody's in."

(82)

The four of the haiku quoted above describe jazz performance in terms of a pair of chopsticks. In his notes Emanuel remarks, "Chops and Twin are names given to the chopsticks (Chops the slower, sturdier one, Twin the roaming, more imaginative one)" (82). The pair plays the roles of bow and arrow: if they do not work together, they fall and fail to capture what they desire. The pair is in unison with the music, Chops making "drum sounds SPIN" and Twin coaxing them, herding them in. Jazz would not be inspirational if only one individual played the music: Chops's role is as important as Twin's. Jazz captures life as though the pair "harpoons the whale": while "Chops runs the scale," "Twin slides loose." And jazz music intensifies with a coordination of bass and melody, a pair of chopsticks.

Emanuel's admonition for African Americans to be individualistic in their lives is remindful of Zen doctrine. The concept of subjectivity in Zen, however, goes a step further, for it calls for a severe critique of self. The doctrine of satori calls for the follower to annihilate self to reach the higher state of *mu* so as to liberate self from the habitual way of life. In Zen, one must destroy not only self-centeredness and intellectualism, but God, Buddha, Christ, any prophet, or any idol because it is only the self, no one else, that can deliver the individual to the state of *mu*. Emanuel urges the liberation of self and the destruction of injustice in such jazz haiku as "Jackhammer," and "Ammunition," and "Impressionist":

Jackhammer Jazz POUNDS—
just breathes—on your door. Message:
don't lock it no more.

Weapons ready-y-y. JAZZ!
People fall, rise hypnotized,
maybe civilized.

Impressionist pipe
puffs JAZZ where pigments solo,
brightsoapbubbling air.

(70)

Each poem focuses on the sound of jazz that inspires the liberation of self from the ways one has been conditioned to lead. Jazz pounds away the door of racism. Jazz is an ammunition to destroy barbarism: people will "fall, rise hypnotized, / maybe civilized." Through its impressionist pipe, jazz creates "brightsoapbubbling air," a colorful, exciting new world.

The liberation of self which jazz inspires is akin to the concept of liberation in Zen. Zen teaches its followers to liberate themselves from human laws, rules, and authorities. For jazz, as for Zen, liberation results from one's desire to adhere to the law and spirit of nature. In a haiku on "The Rabbit Capers," which resembles a *senryu,*[22]

White Bugsy Rabbit
went scratch-scratch-scratch: jailed for theft
from The Old Jazz Patch.

(78)

the jazz caper is portrayed as a work of art that is created for its own sake: the jazzrabbit, in another haiku, "aims his gun, shoots / . . . just for fun" (78). For Emanuel, jazz inspires one, as does Zen, with a new way of life: jazz and Zen admonish one to purge one's mind and heart of any materialistic thoughts and feelings, and appreciate the wonder of life here and now.

Jazz, as Emanuel remarks in his preface, "has crossed oceans and continents to spread its gospel of survival through joy and artistic imagination" (v). Throughout *Jazz from the Haiku King* he is intent upon composing haiku on the basis of its well-established philosophical and aesthetic principles. Philosophically, his finely wrought haiku enlighten the reader as inspiring jazz does the listener. Aesthetically as well, Emanuel's haiku, sharing the devices of both haiku and jazz by which to seize the moments of revelation, express natural, spontaneous sentiments. His haiku, with sharp, compressed images, strongly reflect the syncopated sounds and rhythms of African American Jazz.

NOTES

1. See William Higginson, *Haiku Handbook* (New York: McGraw-Hill, 1985), 49–51.

2. See Kenneth Yasuda, *Japanese Haiku* (Rutland, VT: Charles Tuttle, 1957), xvii.

3. Higginson, *Haiku Handbook* 51.

4. Ibid., 63–64.

5. See Harold G. Henderson, *Introduction to Haiku: An Anthology of Poems and Poets from Basho to Shiki* (New York: Doubleday/Anchor, 1958), x.

6. Higginson, *Haiku Handbook* 65.

7. Michel Fabre, *Unfinished Quest of Richard Wright* (New York: Morrow, 1973), 505. This poet was later identified as Sinclair Beiles, a South African beats poet who was living in Paris as was Wright.

8. Ibid., 505.

9. Ibid., 506.

10. Ibid., 508–9.

11. See Constance Webb, *Richard Wright: A Biography* (New York: Putnam, 1968), 387, 393–94.

12. 817 haiku were published in *Haiku: This Other World*; 3,183 haiku, the rest of the 4,000 in the posthumous manuscript "Four Thousand Haiku," remain unpublished.

13. The original in Japanese reads "Yama-dori-no | o | wo | fumu | haru no | iri-hi | kana" (Henderson 102).

14. The original of this haiku by Basho is in Henderson 40.

15. See *Haiku: This Other World*. The 817 haiku are numbered consecutively, as noted earlier: "In the Silent Forest" is 316 and "A Thin Waterfall" 569.

16. The word *sabi* in Japanese, a noun, derives from the verb *sabiru*, to rust, implying that what is described is aged, as discussed in Chapter 1. Buddha's portrait hung in Zen temples, the old man with a thin body, is nearer to his soul as the old tree with its skin and leaves fallen is nearer to the very origin and essence of nature. For a further discussion of Buddha's portrait, see Loehr 216.

17. As discussed earlier, while Freud defines death as the opposite of life, meaning that death reduces all animate things to the inanimate. Lacan defines death as "human experience, human interchanges, intersubjectivity," suggesting that death is part of life (*Seminar* 2: 80). To Lacan, the death instinct is not "an admission of impotence, it isn't a coming to a halt before an irreducible, an ineffable last thing, it is a concept" (*Seminar* 2: 70).

18. This stanza, filled with rather superficial racial and cultural labels, is reminiscent of the least inspiring stanza in Whitman's "Song of Myself":

Magnifying and applying come I, Outbidding at the start the old cautious hucksters,
Taking myself the exact dimensions of Jehovah,
Lithographing Kronos, Zeus his son, and Hercules his grandson,
Buying drafts of Osiris, Isis, Belus, Brahma, Buddha,
In my portfolio placing Manito loose, Allah on a leaf, the crucifix engraved,
With Odin and the hedeous-faced Mexitli and every idol and image,

                                              (Whitman, *Complete Poetry* 58)

19. The first collection of *renga*, *Chikuba Kyogin Shu* (*Chikuba Singers' Collection*, 1499) includes over two hundred *tsukeku* (adding verses) linked with the first verses of another poet. As the title of the collection suggests, the salient characteristic of *renga* (linked song) was a display of ingenuity and coarse humor.

20. Craig Werner has provided an incisive account of the jazz impulse: "Jazz, observed Louis Armstrong, is music that's never played the same way once. The world changes, the music changes. Jazz imagines the transitions, distills the deepest meanings of the moment we're in, how it developed from the ones that came before, how it opens up into the multiple possibilities of the ones to come" (*Change* 132).

21. In "A Sight in Camp in the Daybreak Gray and Dim" (*Complete Poetry* 219), an elegy for the dead soldiers, Whitman, as noted earlier, celebrates their death and alludes to their natural and divine heritage.

22. *Senryu* is a humorous haiku. *Senryu* as a poetic genre thrives on moralizing nuances and a philosophical tone that expresses the incongruity of things rather than their oneness. Because *senryu* tend to appeal more to one's sense of the logical than to intuition, this jazz haiku can be read as a *senryu*.

Chapter 6

Kerouac's Haiku and Classic Haiku Poetics

The theory of haiku composition Kerouac acquired from Blyth is based on the three Eastern philosophies: the Buddhist ontology, Zen, and Confucianism. Blyth shows with classic haiku that the Buddhist ontology buttresses what he calls "the theory of transmigration."[1] Buddhists, unlike Christians, believe that both humans and nonhumans possess the soul and that the soul transmigrates between humans and nonhumans. Buddhists thus believe in reincarnation. In depicting animals and insects, classic haiku poets show respect for their lives as equally as for those of human beings.[2] Many of the haiku written in the seventeenth and eighteenth centuries depict animals and insects as those that possess the soul. The poet not only shows them respect but, as a Buddhist, also has compassion on them.

Among the classic haiku poets, Issa wrote many haiku in which he expressed profound respect and sympathy to nonhumans. Issa was a Buddhist priest as well as a haiku poet. His haiku reflect the Buddhist ontology. Ontology is the branch of metaphysics that deals with the nature of being and with the relationships among human beings and nonhuman beings. Issa believed in the equality of humans and nonhumans. Consider the following haiku by Issa:

"Do not Hit the Fly"

Do not hit the fly,
It is praying with its hands
And with its feet.[3]

"By Striking the Fly"

> By striking the fly
> A plant with flowering petals
> Has also been struck.[4]

"Bringing up the Silkworms"

> Bringing up the silkworms,
> They call them
> "Mister."[5]

As these haiku show, Issa makes no clear-cut distinction between humans and nonhumans. As Blyth has observed, "The scale of beings in the Buddhist universe puts man midway. The primitive animistic ideas of the Japanese fall in with the Buddhist system, and all are united by the theory of transmigration. The result is (or is it the cause?) that our sympathies are widened in both directions."[6]

As the following haiku illustrate, nonhumans have the soul. Issa's and Basho's haiku depict the silkworms and octopuses as though they were human beings:

> Bringing up the silkworms,
> They call them
> "Mister."
>
> [*Samazuke ni*
> *Sodate-raretaru*
> *Kaiko kana*]

(Issa, *Haiku* 19)

> The octopuses in the jars:
> Transient dreams
> Under the summer moon.

(Basho, *Haiku* 22)

In Issa's haiku in Japanese, the word *Sama*, translated as "Mister," implies respect for the silkworms. Since *Sama* is used in Japan to call a man or woman, the person addressed with *Sama* is respected as a human being, not as a man. Based on the Buddhist ontology, which does not distinguish between man and woman, addressing the silkworms with *Sama* also implies pious feeling toward them. In Basho's haiku, the image of the octopuses in the jars not only is an image in the poet's imagination but becomes a scene of reality. The reader is convinced that the octopuses have dreams just as do humans.

Not only does the Buddhist ontology underlie the theory of transmigration between humans and nonhumans, its doctrine is extended to the transmigration between the animate and the inanimate. The following haiku by Basho show the transmigration of the soul between humans and plants:

> Yield to the willow
All the loathing, all the desire
> Of your heart.

> [*Moro moro no*
Kokoro yanagi ni
> *Makasu beshi*]

> The lotuses in the pond,
Just as they are, unplucked:
> The Festival of the Dead.

> [*Hasu-ike ya*
Orade sonomama
> *Tamamatsuri*]

(Blyth, *Haiku* 22)

In both haiku, the willow and lotuses and humans are all portrayed as equal beings. The willow has the similar emotion and desire as do the poet and reader of this haiku. The lotuses are holding their festival of the dead in the pond as are the people in the village.

The doctrine that the inanimate and inanimate have the soul admonishes its followers to have mercy on them. Kobayashi Issa (1762–1826), a Buddhist priest, as well as a celebrated haiku poet of his time, followed the doctrine and its admonition. Issa is best known for his famous haiku:

You dare not strike him!
The fly is praying with hands
And praying with feet.

(Translation by Hakutani)

[*Yare utsu na*
Hai ga te wo suru
Ashi wo suru]

Kerouac, fascinated by the Buddhist doctrine of mercy and compassion, wrote the following haiku:

Shall I say no?
> —fly rubbing
Its back legs

(*Book of Haikus* 78)

This haiku suggests that Kerouac wrote it in praise of Issa's haiku. Interestingly, Kerouac wrote another haiku on a fly:

Shall I break God's commandment?
    Little fly
Rubbing its back legs

                                                                (Book of Haikus 109)

By invoking God's Commandment, Kerouac is conflating the Christian teaching with the Buddhist doctrine of mercy, which his other haiku "Shall I Say No?" conveys.

Issa also wrote the following haiku to demonstrate the Buddhist theory of transmigration of the soul, as well as the Buddhist doctrine of mercy and compassion:

        Striking the fly,
I hit also
        A flowering plant.

        [*Hae uchi ni*
Hana saku kusa mo
        Utare keri]

                                                                (Blyth, *Haiku* 227)

        For you flees too,
The night must be long,
        It must be lonely.

        [*Nomi-domo mo*
Yonaga darō zo
        Sabishi karo]

                                                                (Blyth, *Haiku* 306)

"Striking the Fly" not only betrays that the soul exists in the fly and flowing plant, but also admonishes Issa that he has failed to put into practice the doctrine of mercy and compassion. "For You Flees Too" conveys Issa's thought that, though flees are pests to humans, they live their innocent lives just as do innocent humans. In this haiku, an expression of loneliness, a major theme in classic haiku, is intensified by imagining the loneliness of the flees.

As the Buddhist ontology underlies much of classic haiku, Zen philosophy has fascinated many artists and philosophers alike in the East over the centuries. Blyth shows with numerous haiku quoted throughout the volumes that the Zen state of mind underlies many of classic haiku. A haiku poet such as Basho strived to create a vision in which nature and humanity are united. Such a poet sought to suppress individuality and achieve the state of Zen Blyth calls "a state of absolute spiritual poverty in which, having nothing, we possess all"[7] In Zen-inspired haiku, the material or the concrete is emphasized without the expression of any general principle of abstract reasoning. In classic haiku, animate and inanimate lose their differences, so that one might say haiku are not about human beings but about objects in nature. Zen teaches that the ordinary thing and the love of nature are reduced to a detached love of life as it is without idealistic, moralistic, or ethical attachments. Things in nature are equal to those in humanity; both exist through and because of each other. In a Zen-inspired haiku the poet tries to annihilate one's thoughts or feelings before *satori* is attained. *Satori* is the achievement of a state of *mu*, nothingness. The state of nothingness is free of human subjectivity; it is so completely free of any thought or emotion that such a consciousness corresponds to the state of nature.

In the last haiku by Issa quoted earlier ("For you flees too, / The night must be long, / It must be lonely"), human subjectivity is expressed by the third line. The following haiku by Basho and Buson, on the other hand, do not include an expression of human subjectivity:

> The autumn full moon:
> All night long
>> I paced round the lake.

> [*Meigetsu ya*
> *Ike wo megurite*
>> *Yo mo sugara*]

(Basho, Blyth, *Haiku* 294)

> Spreading a straw mat in the field,
> I sat and gazed
>> At the plum blossoms.

> [*Samushiro wo*
> *Hatake ni shiite*
>> *Ume-mi kana*]

(Buson, Blyth, *Haiku* 294)

Basho's haiku simply portrays an autumnal scene at night where Basho was looking at the moon and its reflection on the water while walking around the lake. Basho is not expressing any thoughts or feelings. If he thought and felt about the tranquillity of the scene or the beauty of the moon reflected on the water as he composed the haiku, he must have kept his thoughts and feelings to himself. Buson also simply depicts a scene in early spring where he was gazing at the plum blossoms. Buson, an accomplished painter, might have been impressed by the beauty of the plum blossoms and have attempted to paint this flowering tree, but his admiration of the flower is not expressed in the haiku.

As the Buddhist ontology and Zen philosophy influenced the mindset and technique of haiku, Confucianism also made an impact on the poet's world-view. *The Analects*, which comprises Confucius's maxims and parables, has more to do with human life than with the life of a religious figure such as Buddha. Confucian ethics might be defined as a code of honor by which the individual must live in society. It consists of four virtues written in Chinese characters: 仁 (Humanity), 義 (Justice), 忠 (Loyalty), and 孝 (Filial Piety). Such haiku by Basho as the following express Confucian virtues:

> Shake, O grave!
> My wailing voice
> Is the autumn wind.

> [*Tsuka mo ugoke*
> *Waga naku koe wa*
> *Aki no kaze*]

(Basho. Blyth, *Haiku* 82)

> Should I take it in my hand,
> It would disappear with my hot tears,
> Like the frost of autumn.

> [*Te ni toraba*
> *Kien namida zo atsuki*
> *Aki no shimo*]

(Basho, Blyth, *Haiku* 82)

The first haiku, the autumn wind and the wailing voice convey the grief of the poet over his friend's death, a genuine human sentiment and virtue. The second haiku focuses on the tears his mother's death brought; his tears were so hot that his mother's hair would disappear like autumn frost.

As these haiku suggest, Confucian virtues are derived from human senti-ments as well as from natural phenomena. Confucian virtues posit the unity of humanity and nature. Nakae Toju (1608–1648), one of the most influential thinkers in Japanese history, wrote, "Heaven and Earth and man appear to be different, but they are essentially one. This essence has no size, and the spirit of man and the infinite must be one."[8] Toju's view of humanity and nature echoes Confucius's worldview. For Confucius, God is not a living being like a human being: God is a concept that originates from a human being. The individual living in society thus formulates this concept by apprehending the ways of nature in heaven and on earth. God, then, reflects the conscience, a code of ethics established by the individual. Confucius sees one who is endowed with ethics, a virtuous man, is able to establish one's conscience. If a man is without virtues, on the other hand, neither can he conceal his nature nor can he rest peacefully in his life.

In *Analects* 8. 8, Confucius urges the reader to:

Arise with poetry;
Stand with propriety;
Grow with music[9]

"The mind," Blyth remarks, "is roused by poetry, made steadfast by propriety, and perfected by music." *Analects* 9. 16 reads: "Standing by a stream, Confucius said, 'It ceases not day or night, flowing on and on like this.'"[10] Not only is Confucius's description of the scene poetic and beautiful to look at, it also conveys universal truth.

The Analects emphasizes the ultimate truth, the fixed, immutable principles of the universe. Some of Basho's haiku express the inevitability of whatever happens in human life, as well as the active acceptance of the inevitable. The following haiku by Basho show the irreversible way of the universe to which a living being must conform:

A flower of the camellia-tree
Fell,
Spilling its water.

[*Ochizama ni*
Mizu koboshi keri
Hana-tsubaki]

(Blyth, *Haiku* 10)

The year draws to its close;
But I am still wearing
My *kasa* and straw sandals.

[*Toshi kurenu*
Kasa kite waraji
Hakinagara]

(Blyth, *Haiku* 171)

"A Flower of the Camellia-Tree" shows the inevitability of natural phenomena: a flower fades as its water falls to the ground. "The Year Draws to Its Close," while describing the passing of a year, also suggests that, even though the poet wearing his hat and sandals finds himself on the road, his journey must come to a close.

For the technique of haiku, Blyth takes up various subjects, such as humor, simplicity, brevity, syllabic measure, and seasonal reference. Humor and simplicity have more to do with matter than manner. They are essential parts of the content of haiku, the underling philosophies expressed in the haiku. Humor, in particular, seems hardly part of haiku, what Blyth calls "some poise of the mind, some balance of conflicting elements from which arises the pleasure whose peculiar quality causes us to give it the name of humour."[11] A classic haiku with humor thrives on the brevity of expression as the saying, "Brevity is the soul of wit," implies. Some of Wright's haiku with humor are composed with the poise of the mind. Not only do Wright's haiku adhere to the syllabic count of 5, 7, 5, but many of his haiku with humor come alive with terse, compressed expressions and images.

"This 5, 7, 5," Blyth sees, "has a wave-like character of flow, suspense and ebb, it is symmetrical, yet in odd numbers."[12] Haiku translated into English, as shown in Blyth's volumes, do not and cannot abide by the syllabic requirement, for words in English tend to be longer than those in Japanese. Classic and modern haiku in Japan all adhere to the syllabic rule, though some haiku poets, including Basho, have written with anomalous syllabic counts. Even Basho's famous haiku "On a Withered Branch" has two versions with different syllabic sequences. The earlier version "Kare eda ni / Karasu no tomari taru ya / Aki no kure" (Imoto 86) has a syllabic sequence of 5, 10, 5, while the later version "Kare-eda ni / Karasu-no tomari-keri / Aki-no-kure" (Hernderson 18) has 5, 9, 5 syllables, both in an unusual pattern. Such anomalies in Japanese haiku, however, are extremely rare exceptions.

It is remarkable that Richard Wright strictly followed the 5, 7, 5 syllabic measure in composing haiku. Of the four thousand haiku he wrote, only a fraction of them, perhaps less than one percent, were composed with anomalous syllabic counts. Yone Noguchi and Ezra Pound both ignored the rule. So did Jack Kerouac. Most of the contemporary poets who tried their hand at haiku, such as Sonia Sanchez and Lenard D. Moore, do not follow the rule, either. James Emanuel, whose haiku have been discussed earlier, strictly followed the rule. Wright's application of the syllabic rule in classic haiku to English haiku in an attempt to create the haiku rhythm in English was an achievement in itself.

The brevity of expression in haiku is accomplished by other techniques such as seasonal reference and cutting word. In classic haiku, as well as in modern haiku in Japan, a seasonal word, *kigo*, is required. "This word," Blyth notes, "may give the atmospheric background, it may be a kind of seed, a trigger which releases a whole world of emotion, of sounds and scents and colours. It is thus a form of brevity, so that when we say 'the moon,' we mean the full moon of autumn."[13]

Conventionally, a letter in Japanese begins with a seasonal greeting and a reference to weather. This custom may have derived from the poets of the Muromachi period (1392–1573) who perceived the season in each climatic, environmental, and biological phenomenon—spring rain, winter snow, cherry blossoms, falling leaves, autumn sunset, the harvest moon, and the like by which it became a literary representation. A seasonal word gives each haiku a vastness and universality it might not ordinarily have. This reference gives the poem a sense of infinity and eternity as it itself remains finite and temporary. In addition, the *kigo* serves an aesthetic function since it has a capacity to evoke commonly perceived images of beauty. Buson's "Also Stepping On" uses the spring setting sun for the *kigo*: "Also stepping on / The mountain pheasant's tail is / The spring setting sun" (*Yama-dori-no / O wo fumu haru no / Iri-hi kana."*[14] Seasonal words are often associated with certain conventional perceptions and implications. Morning glories, for example, evoke the thought of quickly fading beauty, autumn winds imply loneliness and sadness, and plum blossoms suggest that they are merely precursors of perfect beauty to be created by later cherry blossoms.

The following haiku by Basho shows that a *kigo* unifies and condenses expression:

On a withered branch
A crow has just perched
Autumn evening.[15]

(Basho)

In the haiku, "Autumn," a single word, contributes to the unity and brevity of expression. Basho depicts a crow that has just perched on a withered branch, a moment of reality at present. This image is followed by the coming of an autumn night fall, a feeling of future. Present and future, each defining the other, are united.

The use of cutting word, *kireji*, also has the effect of shortening and unifying expression. The classic *renga* (linked verse) had eighteen varieties of *kireji* for dividing its sections: *ya, kana, keri*, etc. Basho increased the variety to forty-eight as the use of *kireji* was redefined and expanded. In "The Old Pond," mentioned earlier, the syllable *ya* is attached to the words *furu ike* (old pond): Basho is expressing a feeling of awe about the quietude of the pond. In another famous haiku, Basho used *ya* to emphasize the deadly quiet atmosphere of the woods he visited: "It's deadly quiet: / Piercing into the rocks

/ Is the shrill of cicada" (*"Shizu kesa ya / Iwa ni shimi iru / Semi no koe"*).
Above all, adding a *kireji* is a structural device to "cut" or divide a whole
into parts. Since composing a haiku is confined to seventeen syllables in three
lines, the parts of a vision or idea must be clearly segmented and united in its
development. Dividing the whole into its sections, in turn, gives the section
with a *kireji* much weight. The use of cutting words in haiku thus signifies the
poet's conviction about a natural phenomenon with which he or she is struck.
Because the poet's response to the scene is interpreted as decisive, the overall
vision created in the poem is further clarified. Traditionally, cutting words
convey one's hope, wish, demand, call, question, resignation, awe, wonder,
surprise, and the like.

Kerouac substituted English punctuation marks for cutting words. For
example, the dash (—) at the end of the first line is a substitute for the cutting
word, *ya*, a sigh of a beautiful scene:

Perfect moonlit night—
    marred
By family squabbles

                               (*Book of Hakus* 17)

River wonderland—
    The emptiness

                              (*Book of Haikus* 100)

Spring evening—
    Hobo with hard on
Like bamboo

                              (*Book of Haikus* 144)

The cows of Autumn—
    laughing along the fence,
Roosters at Dawn

                              (*Book of Haikus* 174)

Kerouac sometimes used the comma (,) as a substitute for the cutting word
kana for putting emphasis or expressing surprise:

This July evening,
    A large frog
On my doorsill

                              (*Book of Haikus* 18)

Rainy night,
> the top leaves wave
In the gray sky

> > > (*Book of Haikus* 64)

Desolation, Desolation,
> so hard
To come down off of

> > > (*Book of Haikus* 98)

Onomatopoeia is another technique seen in some Japanese haiku. "Of all languages," as Blyth noted, "Japanese is by far the richest in onomatopoetic elements, especially of the simpler variety, in which the sound of the word is directly an imitation of the thing."[16] The following by Buson and Issa sound lively because of the repetition of certain syllables in Japanese, as well as in English translation:

> "Day, ah, darken day!
Night, ah, dawn away!"
> Chant the frogs.

> [*Hi wa hi kure yo*
Yo wa yo ake yo to
> *Naku kaeru*]

> > > (Buson)

> The spring sea,
Gently rising and falling,
> The whole day long.

> [*Haru no umi*
Hine mosu notari
> *Norari kana*]

> > > (Buson)

> Waveringly,
A huge firefly
> passes buy.

> [*Ō botaru*
Yurari yurari to
> *Tōri keri*]
> > (Issa)

> > > (Blyth, *Haiku* 321–23)

The first haiku by Buson has alliterations of *"Hi"* and *"hi kure"* and *"yo"* and *"yoake"*; the English version has an alliteration of "Day," "darken," and "day." In Buson's second haiku, *"notari"* in the second line is repeated in the third line as the second line in the English version has a repetitious present participle "rising" and "falling." In Issa's haiku, *"yurari"* is repeated in the first line as the three lines all end with the "y" sound.

Some of Kerouac's haiku have alliterations as the following show:

The crickets—crying
        for rain—
Again

(Book of Haikus 23)

Dawn—crows cawing,
        ducks quack quacking,
Kitchen windows lighting

(Book of Haikus 50)

A big fat lake
        of snow
Falling all alone

(Book of Haikus 54)

Rig rig rig—
        that's the rat
On the roof

(Book of Haikus 92)

Each of the haiku is highlighted by the repetition of sounds: "the crickets—crying," "crow cawing ," "ducks quack quacking," "fat flake . . . Falling," "Rig rig rig," "the rat / On the roof." This repetition of sounds is similar to that in the following haiku:

Dragonflies fly, —
Above them too fly dragonflies, —
        In the dragonfly sky.[17]

        [*Tombo tobu*
Tombo no ue mo
        Tombo tobu sora]

Analogy is another technique of haiku closely related to the function of onomatopoeia. While the repetition of sounds is directly representative of the objects or phenomena depicted, analogy itself, as Blyth notes, "is always indirect, unconscious, spontaneous. Great Poetry depends chiefly for its effect upon this factor. It cannot be imitated or artificially produced."[18] In the following haiku the analogy drawn is indirect but spontaneous:

> The people are few
> A few leaves are falling too
> Now and then.[19]

> [*Hito chirari*
> *Konoha mo chirari*
> *Horari kana*]

(Issa)

> Do not doubt it,
> The bay has its spring too,—
> The flowers of the tide.[20]

> [*Utagau na*
> *Ushio no hana mo*
> *Ura no haru*]

(Basho)

> Slow days passing, accumulating,—
> How distant they are,
> The Things of the past![21]

> [*Osoki hi no*
> *Tsumorite tōki*
> *Mukashi kana*]

(Buson)

Issa's haiku draws an analogy between people and leaves, Basho's between spring flowers and spring tides, Buson's between present and past, each relation subtly and spontaneously expressed. Even though the analogy is drawn by the poet, his view is concealed and subjectivity is absent in the haiku.

Because haiku is limited in its length, it must achieve its effect through an internal unity and harmony. The unity of sentiment in haiku can be depicted through the transference of the senses. Basho's "Sunset on the Sea," for example, shows the unity and relatedness of the senses:

Sunset on the sea:
The voices of the ducks
Are faintly white.[22]

[*Umi kurete*
Kamo no koe hono
Ka ni shiroshi]

(Basho)

The voices of the ducks under the darkened sky are delineated as white as well as faint. The chilled wind after dark evokes the whiteness associated with coldness. The voices of the ducks and the whiteness of the waves refer to entirely different senses, but both senses, each reinforcing the other, create a unified sensation.

In Buson's haiku, the transference of the senses occur between color and another sense, as shown in these:

In the moonlight
The colour and scent of the wisteria blossoms
        Seem far away.

    [*Tsuki ni tōku*
Oboyuru fuji no
        Iroka kana]

(Buson)

    Happiness,
At the white face of the child
        In the small mosquito net.[23]

    [*Kao shiroki*
Ko no ureshisa yo
        Makura-gaya]

(Buson)

In the first haiku, the color and scent of the wisteria blossoms under the moonlight unify the sentiment expressed. The haiku of Buson, a painter as well as a poet, are often pictorial. In this haiku, color is linked not only to scent but to distance. In the second haiku, the transference is between color and feeling, the child's white face and happiness.

Not only did Kerouac learn the specific techniques of haiku composition from classic haiku, he also learned the most important philosophical state of mind that underlines haiku, called *mu*. A Zen-inspired poet suppresses human subjectivity as much as possible, or minimize it, in depicting an object or a phenomenon in nature. This poetic perspective rids the poet of egotism and self-centerdness. Kerouac also learned from classic haiku poets like Issa the Buddhist theory of transmigration. Christianity, with which Kerouac grew up, regarded nonhumans like animals and birds as lesser or lower than humans. In Buddhism, nonhuman beings are equal to human beings and both species possess the soul, which is shared as we coexist in life and death. All in all, classic haiku taught Kerouac that not only must human beings treat their fellow human beings with compassion, but they must also treat nonhuman beings as their equals. Classic haiku showed the worldview that human beings are not at the center of the universe.

NOTES

1. Blyth, *Haiku* 19.
2. As Blyth notes, "There is also no clear-cut distinction between human and sub-human. The scale of beings in the Buddhist universe puts man midway. The primitive animistic ideas of the Japanese fall in with the Buddhist system, and all are united by the theory of transmigration. The result is (or is it the cause?) that our sympathies are widened in both directions" (*Haiku* 19).
3. The translation is by Hakutani.
4. Ibid.
5. Blyth, *Haiku* 19. The translation of this haiku is by Blyth.
6. Blyth, *Haiku* 19.
7. Ibid., 162.
8. Ibid., 80.
9. Ibid., 72.
10. Ibid., 72.
11. Ibid., 313.
12. Ibid., 329.
13. Ibid., 335.
14. Henderson, 102.
15. The translation of this haiku is by Hakutani.
16. Blyth, *Haiku* 321.
17. Ibid., 327.
18. Ibid., 324.
19. Ibid., 326. The translation of Issa's haiku is by Hakutani.
20. Ibid., 326. The translation of Basho's haiku is by Blyth.
21. Ibid., 326. The translation of Buson's haiku is by Blyth.
22. Imoto 117. The translation of Basho's haiku is by Hakutani.
23. Blyth, *Haiku* 301. The translation of Buson's haiku is by Blyth.

Chapter 7

Kerouac's Haiku and Beat Poetics

Jack Kerouac (1922–1969), whose novel *On the Road* (1957) captured a huge audience, played a central role in the literary movement he named the Beat Generation. His other novel *The Dharma Bums* (1958) gave an intimate biographical account of himself in search of the truths in life. In San Francisco he met Gary Snyder (1930–) and the two Dharma bums explored the thoughts and practices of Buddhism. As Snyder left for Japan to study at a Zen monastery, Kerouac's search reached an apogee on a desolate mountain top in the Sierras.

The uninhibited story of Kerouac and Snyder on the West Coast also coincided with the birth of the San Francisco Poetry Renaissance. Kerouac called the event "the whole gang of howling poets" gathered at Gallery Six on October 7, 1955, as described in the beginning of *The Dharma Bums*.[1] Not only did this inaugural meeting of the Beat Generation feature the three well-known writers Kerouac, Snyder, and Ginsberg (1926–1997), their subsequent interactions among them revealed their backgrounds and worldviews. Snyder (1930–), born in San Francisco, followed Ginsberg's first reading of *Howl* at this gathering with his own lyrical poems, as mentioned above. Later in *The Dharma Bums* Snyder observed: "Think of millions of guys all over the world with rucksacks on their backs tramping around the back country and hitchhiking and bringing the word down to everybody." Kerouac responded by referring to a Christian tradition he remembered as he grew up a Catholic in a French-Canadian family in Massachusetts.

Discussing Buddhism and Zen philosophy, in particular, with Snyder, as well as reading books on Buddhism in the local libraries, Kerouac realized that Buddhism, rather than denying suffering and death, confronted both. For him, Buddhism taught one to transcend the origin of suffering and death: desire and ignorance. Most impressively, Buddhism taught Kerouac that

111

the phenomenal world was like a dream and an illusion and that happiness consisted in achieving that strange vision in the mind—enlightenment. *The Dharma Bums* also informs that while Snyder was continuously fascinated with Zen, Kerouac was inspired by Mahayana Buddhism. To Kerouac, Zen, which teaches spontaneous, realistic action for human beings, compromises with active, worldly existence. Kerouac, impressed with Mahayana Buddhism, believed that one's goal of life is to achieve Buddhahood, a celestial state of enlightenment and acceptance of all forms of life.

During this period Kerouac, immersed with American transcendentalism, read Emerson, Thoreau, and Whitman. Kerouac was influenced by Emerson's concept of self-reliance as he learned of Whitman's singular, stubborn independence and refusal to subscribe to society's materialistic, commercial demands. At the same time it was Thoreau's writings, such as *Walden*, *A Week on the Concord and Merrimack Rivers*, and "Civil Disobedience" that introduced Kerouac to Confucianism and Buddhism.[2]

Learning about Buddhism from Thoreau, Kerouac became seriously interested in studying its philosophy. His study of Buddhism, then, led to writing *The Dharma Bums*. For Kerouac, Mahayana Buddhism served to change the state of defeat in the world that the Beat movement represented to the beatific acceptance of life the Buddhist texts described. For Gary Snyder, Zen Buddhism transformed the Beats to the Zen Lunatics who refused "to subscribe to the general demand that they consume production and therefore have to work for the privilege of consuming, all that crap they didn't really want anyway such as refrigerators, TV sets, cars . . . . I see a vision of . . . Zen Lunatics who go about writing poems that happen to appear in their heads for no reason and also by being kind and also by strange unexpected acts keep giving visions of eternal freedom to everybody and to all living creatures" (*Dharma Bums* 97–98).

Kerouac responded, as did Snyder, to the Zen principle to establish authority in one's spontaneous and intuitive insights and actions. Kerouac took pains to see things as they existed without commentary, interpretation, and judgment. For Kerouac, and for the Beat Generation, the Zen perspective made art conform to life itself. A Zen-inspired poet must see whatever happens in life—order and disorder, permanence and change. This Zen principle partly accounts for Kerouac's rejection of the idea of revision.[3] With respect to spontaneous prose, Kerouac stated: "And, Not 'selectivity' of expression but following free deviation (association) of mind into limitless blow-on-subject seas of thought, . . . write as deeply, fish down as far as you want, satisfy yourself first, then reader cannot fail to receive telepathic shock and meaning—excitement by same laws operating in his own human mind."[4]

Upon publication of *On the Road*, Kerouac was writing haiku. Thanks to Regina Weinreich's edition, *Book of Haikus* by Jack Kerouac (2003), we have a well-detailed account of Kerouac's writing of those several hundred haiku. As mentioned in *The Dharma Bums*, Kerouac, while reading a number of books on Buddhism, also consulted the four volume book on Japanese haiku by R. H. Blyth, especially the first volume, subtitled "Eastern Culture." "Kerouac's pocket notebooks," as Weinreich notes, contained "haiku entries written in New York City, Tangier, Aix-en-Provence, London, New York City again, Berkeley, Mexico, and Orlando. As the notebooks and letters of this period show, Kerouac exhorted himself to write haiku, mindful of the traditional methods" (*Book of Haikus* 106).

As Kerouac's *Book of Haikus* indicates, Kerouac continuously wrote haiku to render the Beats' worldview. "For a new generation of poets," Weinreich has observed, "Kerouac ended up breaking ground at a pioneering stage of an American haiku movement" (*Book of Haikus* xv). Allen Ginsberg celebrated Kerouac's haiku: "Kerouac has the one sign of being a great poet, which is he's the only one in the United States who knows how to write haikus. Whereas Kerouac thinks in haikus, every time he writes anything—talks that way and thinks that way. So it's just natural for him."[5] There were, however, some poets who were not enthusiastic about Kerouac's haiku. Lawrence Ferlinghetti, who were associated with the Beat writers and the San Francisco Renaissance poets and who, founding his own press, published his friend Allen Ginsberg's work, said that Kerouac "was a better novel writer than a poem writer."[6]

As many of the classic haiku poets in Japan like Basho were influenced by Confucian thought, so was Kerouac. In the first volume, *Haiku: Eastern Culture*, which Kerouac studied in earnest, Blyth explains that, according to Confucius, the universe consists of heaven, earth, and human beings. *The Analects*, a collection of Confucian maxims and parables, contains Confucius's thoughts and observations on the relationships among heaven, human beings, and God. For Confucius, God is not a living being like a human being: God is a concept that originated from a human being. The individual living in society must formulate this concept by apprehending the ways of nature in heaven and on earth. One is conscious of the supremacy of heaven over earth and human beings.

Several of Kerouac's haiku reflect a Confucian perspective that all things in the universe are related and united:

The tree looks
    like a dog
Barking at Heaven

                           (*Book of Haikus* 3)

Not only does this piece show the relatedness of a tree, a dog, and Heaven, it intimates the sense that the dog and the tree, the animate and the inanimate, are united. This haiku recalls an illusion expressed in Moritake's haiku, which Ezra Pound quoted in his "Vorticism" essay:[7]

The fallen blossom flies back to its branch:
     A butterfly

("Vorticism" 467)

Another haiku by Kerouac on the same subject,

Shooting star!—no,
          lightning bug!—
ah well, June night

(*Book of Haikus* 151)

also depicts an illusion as does Kerouac's haiku above, "The Tree Looks," both haiku illustrating the Confucian thought that all things in the universe are related.

Some other haiku convey the conflated vision of Confucianism and Buddhism that all the living on earth are related and united:

Frozen
     in the birdbath,
A leaf

(*Book of Haikus* 5)

This piece conveys the Buddhist doctrine that all things, even the inanimate, have the Buddha nature. The reason for Kerouac's stronger attraction to Buddhism than to Christianity was his realization that Buddhists believed in the existence and transmigration of the soul in animals as well as in human beings as Christians did not.[8] Not only are the bird and a leaf in this haiku, "Frozen," related, water and ice unite them as if their souls transmigrate between them.

Still other haiku, while illustrating the Confucian and Buddhist perspective of the world that the animate and the inanimate are united, express irony and humor:

After the shower,
     among the drenched roses,
The bird thrashing in the bath

(*Book of Haikus* 14)

In "After the Shower," while the roses are benefiting from rain water, the bird, thrashing in the water, appears uncomfortable. But from a human point of view, the bird also is benefiting from the rain water, which cleans it as if the bird were taking a bath. In the following piece,

Bee, why are you
        staring at me?
I'm not a flower!

                                        (*Book of Haikus* 15)

Kerouac is expressing the bee's perspective: a flower and a human being are the same, the difference being that a flower might provide a bee with honey whereas a human being might be the bee's enemy. Another piece on the same topic,

Ignoring my bread,
        the bird peeking
In the grass

                                        (*Book of Haikus* 24)

expresses irony, for seeds in the grass for the bird are far more delicious than bread, a representation of human products. Another similar haiku,

Looking for my cat
        in the weeds,
I found a butterfly

                                        (*Book of Haikus* 40)

is ironic and humorous, because humans unexpectedly discover beautiful things in the ugly. The perspectives of nature and humanity differ, those of beauty in particular.

As a Beat writer, Kerouac was inspired by the Zen doctrine that to attain enlightenment is to reach the state of nothingness. Not only is this state of mind free of human subjectivity and egotism, it is even free of religious conception. The Rinzai Zen teaches its followers that if they see Buddha in their meditations, they must "kill" him. At the same time, Kerouac was deeply influenced by Mahayana Buddhism which teaches that one can achieve Buddhahood in life or death and that the human soul, buttressed by the virtues of mercy and compassion, transmigrate from one living to another.

In *The Dharma Bums*, Gary Snyder, a Zen Buddhist, had a dialogue with Kerouac, a Mahayana Buddhist, that revealed the two different religiosities the two branches of Buddhism represented. Snyder said to Kerouac,

"I appreciate your sadness about the world. 'Tis indeed. Look at that party the other night. Everybody wanted to have a good time and tried real hard but we all woke up the next day feeling sorta sad and separate. What do you think about death . . . ?" Kerouac responded: "I think death is our reward. When we die we go straight to nirvana Heaven and that's that" (202). In "On the Beat Generation," an unpublished scroll manuscript, Kerouac wrote, "Beat Generation means a generation passed over into eternity . . . . The last trembling of a leaf, at being one with all time, a sudden brilliance of redness in the fall . . . . The beat generation knows all about haikus."[9] Kerouac's observations of the Beat Generation suggest that the Beat poetics is not to describe the life of the beaten but to celebrate the life of the beatific. For Kerouac, and for the Beat generation, the state of beatitude can be attained in life or death. This haiku,

The bottoms of my shoes
        are clean
From walking in the rain

                                                                (*Book of Haikus* 8)

suggests that, ironically, nature, which is organic, is cleaner than humanity, which is less organic. Likewise this piece on the same topic,

In back of the Supermarket,
        in the parking lot weeds,
Purple flowers

                                                                (*Book of Haikus* 18)

ironically suggesting the supremacy of nature over humanity, contains an image of natural beauty in an unnatural environment. In the following piece,

Glow worms
        brightly sleeping
On my flowers

                                                                (*Book of Haikus* 137)

Kerouac is envious of the glow worms sleeping on his flowers, which are oblivious of the chaotic society of which he is a member. This haiku has an affinity with Frost's "After Apple-Picking," in which Frost is envious of the woodchuck's peaceful hibernation as he is afraid of a nightmare caused by the chaotic world.[10] In this haiku by Kerouac,

Am I a flower
        bee, that you
Stare at me?

                                                                (*Book of Haikus* 155)

the speaker is flattered: to the bee he looks as attractive as a flower, an image of beatitude.

Wandering in the fields and the woods, as Kerouac describes in *The Dharma Bums*, he thought that "the substance of my bones and their bones and the bones of dead men in the earth of rain at night is the common individual substance that is everlastingly tranquil and blissful?" It occurred to him: "Raindrops are ecstasy, raindrops are not different from ecstasy, neither is ecstasy different from raindrops, yea, ecstasy is raindrops, rain on, O cloud!" (110). Many of the haiku collected in his notebooks, "V. 1958–1959: Beat Generation Haikus / Autumn," and "VI. 1960–1966: Northport Haikus / Winter," describe what he called "ecstasy":

The droopy constellation
    on the grassy hill—
Emily Dickinson's Tomb

                                                   (*Book of Haikus* 154)

In enormous blizzard
    burying everything
My cat's out mating

                                                   (*Book of Haikus* 164)

Because the aim of a Beat poet is to reach eternity, the first haiku, "The Droopy Constellation," is reminiscent of Emily Dickinson's poetry. In such a poem as "I Died for Beauty" and "Because I Could Not Stop for Death," Dickinson describes her journey to eternity.[11] In the second haiku, "In Enormous Blizzard," an image of a powerful blizzard burying everything on earth suggests death and eternity, but it is juxtaposed to an image of love-making that suggest life and ecstasy. This piece bears a resemblance to Basho's "The Love of the Cats":

    The love of the cats;
When it was over, the hazy moon
    Over the bed-chamber.[12]

Both of Kerouac's haiku suggest there is ecstasy in life and death, love and eternity.

Kerouac's Beat poetics, based on Zen doctrine, led to his concept of individual freedom. Lying on his bag smoking, as Kerouac describes his experience in *The Dharma Bums*, he thought: "Everything is possible. I am God, I am Buddha, I am imperfect Ray Smith, all at the same time, I am empty space, I am all things. I have all the time in the world from life to life to do what is to do, to do what is done, to do the timeless doing, in finitely perfect within, why cry, why worry, perfect like mind essence and the minds of banana peels" (97). Later, envisioning "the bliss of the Buddha-fields," he wrote: "I saw that my life was a vast glowing empty page and I could do anything I wanted" (117). Earlier in the novel, he also recounts the life of a truck driver who gave him a ride when he was hitchhiking to visit his mother in North Carolina. He found that the driver "had a nice home in Ohio with wife, daughter, Christmas tree, two cars, garage, lawn, lawnmower, but he couldn't enjoy any of it because he really wasn't free" (102).

In his notebook collection, "Beat Generation Haikus, 1958–1959," Kerouac included the following piece, which deals with individual freedom:

Jack reads his book
aloud at nite
—the stars come out.

(Book of Haikus 133)

This haiku challenges the Zen concept of *mu* and asserts human subjectivity. Declaring his own ideas, Kerouac is able to find his audience. His call and the stars' response suggest that his vision of the world is as objective as the world's vision of him is subjective. Such a haiku is reminiscent of Robert Frost's poem "The Road Not Taken."[13] Like Frost, Kerouac takes pride in being free and being a nonconformist. The next two pieces also reflect individual freedom and automony:

On Desolation
    I was the alonest man
in the world

(Book of Haikus 136)

High noon
    in Northport
–Alien shore

(Book of Haikus 137)

"On Desolation" and "High Noon" both cherish Kerouac's state of mind dictated by no one but himself. To him, alienation from a corrupt society will lead him to nirvana. Both haiku recall Langston Hughes's "The Weary Blues," in which a Blues musician takes pride in his alienation and autonomy.[14] The following piece, "Reading the Sutra," recounts that the Buddhist scripture inspired Kerouac to attain enlightenment by decisive action on his part:

Reading the sutra
    I decided
To go straight

(Book of Haikus 143)

This haiku has an affinity with Gwendolyn Brooks's "We Real Cool," in which the African American pool players are portrayed as daring individuals who enjoyed living freely on their instincts as did the Beatniks.[15]

Not only are Kerouac's Beat Generation haiku poignant expressions of freedom and individualism, many of them can be read as direct indictments against materialistic society:

Perfect moonlit night
    marred
By family squabble

(Book of Haikus 17)

A quiet Autumn night
    and these fools
Are starting to argue

(177)

Both haiku thrive on the images of celestial beauty. The image of the universe in harmony, however, is juxtaposed to the image of society in conflict. Such a haiku above is in contrast to another Beat Generation haiku:

Ah, the crickets
    are screaming
at the moon

(Book of Haikus 140)

In this piece, the crickets, as they scream at the moon, the preeminent object in the sky, do not quarrel among them. This haiku suggests that human beings, by contrast, at times scream to one another rather than talk about beautiful things on earth and in the sky. In the following haiku,

Desk cluttered
    with mail—
My mind is quiet

(Book of Haikus 145)

despite the image of a cluttered desk representing a chaotic society in which Kerouac lives, the Beat poet is able to attain his peace of mind.

To sum up, then, Kerouac early in his career was well versed in the writings of American transcendentalists, such as Emerson, Thoreau, and Whitman, as well as in Emily Dickinson's poetry. He also found American transcendentalists well acquainted with Confucianism and Buddhism. Through his friendship with such Beat poets as Allen Ginsberg and Gary Snyder, as well as through his studies of Buddhism, Zen, and R. H. Blyth's volume, *Haiku: Eastern Culture* in particular, Kerouac firmly established his poetics. The numerous haiku he wrote reflect his fascination with Mahayana Buddhism, as well as with Zen philosophy. What is remarkable about his haiku is that not only was he influenced by the books he read, he also was inspired by his own experiences in wandering and meditating in the fields and on the mountains.

NOTES

1. Jack Kerouac, *Dharma Bums* (New York: Viking, 1958), 13–14.

2. In *A Week on the Concord and Merrimack Rivers* (1849), Thoreau wrote: "We can tolerate all philosophies, Atomists, Pneumatologists, Atheists, Theoists,—Plato, Aristotle, Leucippus, Democritus, Pythagoras, Zoroaster and Confucius. It is the attitude of these men, more than any communication which they make, that attracts us" (152). In the conclusion of "Civil Disobedience," Thoreau evoked Confucius: "The progress from an absolute to a limited monarchy, from a limited monarchy to a democracy, is a progress toward a true respect for the individual. Even the Chinese philosopher was wise enough to regard the individual as the basis of the empire" (*Variorum Civil Disobedience* 55).

3. John Tytell observes: "Kerouac . . . attacked the concept of revision sacred to most writers as a kind of secondary moral censorship imposed by the unconscious" (*Naked Angels* 17).

4. Jack Kerouac, "Essentials of Spontaneous Prose," *Evergreen Review* 2 (Summer 1958), 73.

5. Tom Lynch, "Intersecting Influences in American Haiku." In *Modernity in East-West Literary Criticism: New Readings*. Edited by Yoshinobu Hakutani (Madison: Fairleigh Dickinson University Press, 2001) 123–24.

6. Barry Gifford and Lawrence Lee, *Jack's Book: An Oral Biography of Jack Kerouac* (New York: St. Martin's, 1978), 271.

7. As noted earlier, Pound quoted Moritake's haiku just before discussing the often quoted poem "In a Station of the Metro": "The apparition of these faces in the crowd: / Petals, on a wet, black bough" ("Vorticism" 48). A literal translation of Moritake's first two lines, "Rak-ka eda ni / Kaeru to mireba," would read: "The fallen blossom appears to come back to its branch." Pound tried to apply the principle of terseness and intensity in Moritake's haiku to the construction of a single image in his poetry. "The 'one image poem,'" Pound noted, "is a form of superposition, that is to say it is one idea set on top of another. I found it useful in getting out of the impasse in which I had been left by my metro emotion" ("Vorticism" 467).

8. Like Thoreau, Kerouac grew up a Christian and was well versed in the Bible but became fascinated with Buddhism. "It is necessary not to be Christian," he argued, "to appreciate the beauty and significance of the life of Christ. I know that some will have hard thoughts of me, when they hear their Christ named beside my Buddha, yet I am sure that I am willing they should love their Christ more than my Buddha" (*A Week* 67).

9. Book of *Haikus* 127.

10. "After Apple-Picking" ends with these lines:

This sleep of mine, whatever sleep it is.
Were he not gone,
The woodchuck could say whether it's like his
Long sleep, as I describe its coming on,
Or just some human sleep.

(Frost's Poems 229)

11. See the last stanza in each poem:

"I died for Beauty"
And so, as Kinsmen, met a Night—
....
And covered up—our name—
"Because I could not stop for Death"
....
I first surmised the Horses' Heads
Were toward Eternity—

(Complete Poems 216, 350)

12. Blyth, *Haiku* 264.

13. See the last stanza of "The Road Not Taken":

I shall be telling this with a sigh
Somewhere ages and ages hence:
Two roads diverged in a wood, and I—
I took the one less traveled by,
And that has made all the difference.

(Frost's Poems 223)

14. See the lines in "The Weary Blues":

In a deep song voice with a melancholy tone
I heard that Negro sing, that old piano moan—
"Ain't got nobody in all this world,
Ain't got nobody but ma self.

(Hughes, Selected Poems 33)

15. See the first two and last two lines in "We Real Cool":

We real cool. We
Left school. We
....
Jazz June. We
Die soon.

(Brooks, Selected Poems 73)

Chapter 8

Kerouac's Haiku and *On the Road*

This autobiographical novel, capturing a huge audience, features himself, named Sal Paradise, as the protagonist and narrator. The story is developed as a quest taken by a young literary aspirant in search of the truths in human life. He has a chief companion on his journey, named Dean Moriarty, whose prototype was Neal Cassady (1926–1968), a major figure of the Beat Generation along with Allen Ginsberg (1926–1997).

For Kerouac, the central mission of *On the Road* is not to describe the life of the beaten but to celebrate the life of the beatific. The narrative turns out to be an experimental novel, for Kerouac himself wants to determine whether he succeeds in achieving that ideal life he has imagined. At the same time he is intent upon finding out whether Dean also succeeds in capturing the life of the beatific. Much like Tom Sawyer in Mark Twain's *Adventures of Huckleberry Finn*, Dean is Sal's friend as well as foil. Kerouac is attracted to him as he is repulsed by him. *On the Road* begins with Kerouac's initial portrait of Dean as a young jailbird who is interested in Nietzsche:

I first met Dean not long after my wife and I split up. I had just gotten over a serious illness that I won't bother to talk about, except that it had something to do with the miserably weary split-up and my feeling that everything was dead. With the coming of Dean Mortiarty began the part of my life you could call my life on the road. Before that I'd often dreamed of going West to see the country, always vaguely planning and never taking off. Dean is the perfect guy for the road because he actually was born on the road, when his parents were passing through Salt Lake City in 1926, in a jalopy, on their way to Los Angeles. First reports of him came to me through Chad King, who'd shown me a few letters from him written in a New Mexico reform school. I was tremendously interested in the letters because they so naïvely and sweetly asked Chad to teach him all about Nietzsche and all the wonderful intellectual things that Chad knew. At one point Carlo [Allen Ginsberg] and I talked about the letters and wondered if we would ever meet the strange Dean Moriarty. (*On the Road* 1)

The mysterious character of Dean Mariarty, whose identity is not revealed in the novel, is compounded by the fact that Neal Cassady was married many times with children, but had a long sexual relationship with Allen Ginsberg.

At the end of the road on the final journey, Kerouac describes his parting with Dean with sadness and compassion:

> Dean took out other pictures. I realized these were all the snapshots which our children would look at some day with wonder, thinking their parents had lived smooth, well-ordered, stabilized-within-the-photo lives and got up in the morning to walk proudly on the side walks of life, never dreaming the raggedy madness and riot of our actual lives, or actual night, the hell of it, the senseless nightmare road. All of it inside endless and beginningless emptiness. Pittiful forms of ignorance. "Good-by, good-by." Dean walked off in the long red dusk. Locomotives smoked and reeled above him. His shadow followed him, it aped his walk and thoughts and very being. He turned and waved coyly, bashfully. He gave me the boomer's high ball, he jumped up and down, he yelled something I didn't catch. He ran around in a circle. All the time he came closer to the concrete corner of the railroad overpass. He made one last signal. I waved back. Suddenly he bent to his life and walked quickly out of sight. (*On the Road* 253–54)

This passage is concluded with a brief description of Kerouac himself: "I gaped into the bleakness of my own days. I had an awful long way to go too" (*On the Road* 254). Such a self-criticism intimates that, although he himself is able to envision the beatific life, his ideal life is beyond reach.

Kerouac's description of the beatific vision of life intensifies because of a contrast drawn between the narrator and his companion. Kerouac introduces himself as Sal Paradise. The word "Paradise" resonates with the Christian heaven, the Garden of Eden. Although Dean is often called "An Angel," he acts like a lost Arch-Angel or a Devil. "I suddenly realized," Kerouac remarks, "that Dean, by virtue of his enormous series of sins, was becoming the Idiot, the Imbecile, the Saint of the lot." Kerouac gives Dean an admonition:

> "You have absolutely no regard for anybody but yourself and your damned kicks. All you think about is what's hanging between your legs and how much money or fun you can get out of people and then you just throw them aside. Not only that but you're silly about it. It never occurs to you that life is serious and there are people trying to make something decent out of it instead of just goofing all the time." (*On the Road* 194)

"That's," utters the narrator, "what Dean was, the HOLY GOOF" (*On the Road* 194). To Kerouac, Dean has transgressed the Christian doctrine of compassion. Dean is antithetical to Kerouac, who tries to achieve a saintly, beatific, and compassionate human life.

In 1957, when Kerouac published *On the Road*, revealing to the literary public his adventures with Neal Cassady and epitomizing the Beat Generation, he wrote many haiku, what Regina Weinreich calls "a fertile group of haiku."[1] While many of these haiku were written in Philip Whalen's cabin in Berkeley, California,[2] they reverberate with *On the Road*. As Kerouac was phrasing the images and ideas for the haiku, he must have been reflecting on his observations of the similar images and ideas that appear in *On the Road*.

Kerouac believed that the central theme of the novel is a spiritual quest of these characters. He was convinced, though his critics did not agree, that the Beat Generation was "basically a religious generation."[3] Some of the Road haiku are expressions of religious thoughts with religious references. Raised by his parents, devout French Catholics, Kerouac makes frequent references to Christianity in general and biblical words in particular.

While, to Kerouac Dean seems to fail in his spiritual quest, he believes Kerouac will succeed in his quest. Envisioning Kerouac's success at the end of the road on the journey, Dean tells Kerouac:

> You spend a whole life of noninterference with the wishes of others, including politicians and the rich, and nobody bothers you and you cut along and make it your own way. . . . What's your road, man?—holyboy road, madman road, rainbow road, guppy road, any road. It's an anywhere road for anybody anyhow. Where body how? (*On the Road* 251)

Dean's listing of "holyboy road" at the top of the various roads suggests that Kerouac will succeed in his spiritual quest because he has strong faith in God. Earlier in the story, Kerouac gives an intimation that his growing up in the East made him a genuine Christian and that his life in the West Coast converted him to a Buddhist. "There is something brown and holy about the East," he says; "and California is white like washlines and emptyheaded—at least that's what I thought then" (*On the Road* 79).[4]

Kerouac's strong faith in Christianity is expressed in several of the group of haiku, "Road Haiku." The following haiku have direct references to Christianity:

Shall I heed God's commandment?
　　　—wave breaking
On the rocks—

　　　　　　　　　　　　　　　　　　　(*Book of Haikus* 109)

A bottle of wine,
       a bishop—
Everything is God

(Book of Haikus 108)

The focus of the first haiku is on Christian doctrine whereas the emphasis in the second haiku is on the concept of pantheism. The second haiku, as does the following haiku, thrives on the concrete images, "a bottle of wine" and "a bishop":

The rose moves
       Like a Reichian disciple
On its stem

(Book of Haikus 121)

Not only does the third haiku have concrete images, "The rose" and "a Reichian disciple," but it also expresses the historical background of the Holy Roman Empire. A pair of haiku that follow depict the images of priests, paying respect not only to the benevolent individuals but also to Christianity as an institution devoted to the welfare of the people:

The vigorous bell-ringing priest
       the catch in the harbor

(Book of Haikus 110)

All these sages
       Sleep
With their mouths open

(Book of Haikus 117)

As both haiku express religious thoughts, the images—the vigorous bell-ringing priest and the sages sleeping with their mouths open—portray the messengers of God and their demeanor as human and humorous as the common people.

At the end of the road in the novel, Kerouac dwells on Christian legend and mythology. During his travels to Mexico he becomes infatuated with Mexican women with Indian heritage. These women are depicted with Biblical references:

"Look at those eyes!" breathed Dean. They were like the eyes of the Virgin Mother when she was a child. We saw in them the tender and forgiving gaze of Jesus. And they stared unflinching into ours. We rubbed our nervous blue eyes and looked again. Still they penetrated us with sorrowful and hypnotic gleam. . . . He stood among them with his ragged face to the sky, looking for the next and highest and final pass, and seemed like the Prophet that had come to them. (*On the Road* 297–98)

The background of this episode is described with Biblical images:

The end of our journey impended. Great fields on both sides of us; a noble wind blew across the occasional immense tree groves and over old missions turning salmon pink in the late sun. The clouds were close and huge and rose. "Mexico City by dusk!" We'd made it, a total of nineteen hundred miles from the afternoon yards of Denver to these vast and Biblical areas of the world, and now we were about to reach the end of the road. (*On the Road* 299)

This portrayal of the Mexican landscape leads to Keouac's speculation on the origin of Adam and Eve:

The waves are Chinese, but the earth is an Indian thing. As essential as rocks in the desert are they in the desert of "history." And they knew this when we passed, ostensibly self-important moneybag Americans on a lark in their land; they knew who was the father and who was the son of antique life on earth, and made no comment. For when destruction comes to the world of "history" and the Apocalypse of the Fellahin returns once more as so many times before, people will still stare with the same eyes from the caves of Mexico as well as from the caves of Bali, where it all began and where Adam was suckled and taught to know. These were my growing thoughts as I drove the car into the hot, sunbaked town of Gregoria. (*On the Road* 280)

From time to time, Kerouac's description of people and their lives on the road are highlighted by Biblical words and expressions, such as "angel," "lamb," and "shepherd." In applauding the jazz performances in Chicago that give him his best times on the road, Kerouac portrays the black musician with a Biblical expression: "Strange flowers yet—for as the Negro alto mused over every one's head with dignity, the young, tall, slender, blond kid from Curtis Street, Denver, jeans and studded belt, sucked on his mouthpiece while waiting for the others to finish; and when they did he started, and you had to look around to see where the solo was coming from, for it came from angelical smiling lips upon the mouthpiece and it was a soft, sweet, fairy-tale solo on an alto. Lonely as America, a throatpierced sound in the night" (*On the Road* 241). Back in Colorado, Kerouac falls in love with a young girl he calls "the prairie angel." "She was about sixteen," he remarks, "and had Plains complexion like wild roses, and the bluest eyes. . . . She stood there with the immense winds that blew clear down from Saskatchewan knocking her hair about her lovely head like shrouds, living curls of them. She blushed and blushed" (*On the Road* 227–28).

On the road to New York from California, Kerouac meets a poor Mexican girl and consummates their love. "We had long, serious talks," he writes, "and took baths and discussed things with the light on and then with the light out. Something was being proved, I was convincing her of something, which she accepted, and we concluded the pact in the dark, breathless, then pleased, like little *lambs*" (*On the Road* 90, emphasis added).

Kerouac's description of the landscape in Mexico as he approaches the end of his journey is reminiscent of the Bible:

> We had reached the approaches of the last plateau. Now the sun was golden, the air keen blue, and the desert with its occasional rivers a riot of sandy, hot space and sudden Biblical tree shade. Now Dean was sleeping and Stan driving. The shepherds appeared, dressed as in first times, in long flowing robes, the women carrying golden bundles of flax, the men staves. Under great trees on the shimmering desert the shepherds sat and convened, and the sheep moiled in the sun and raised dust beyond." (*On the Road* 299)

Kerouac composed some of his Road haiku with Biblical words and expressions:

The Angel's hair
       trailed on my chin
Like a cobweb

                                        (*Book of Haikus* 138)

The bottoms of my shoes
       Are clean
From walking in the rain

                                         (*Book of Haikus* 8)

Kerouac's use of Biblical language is indirect and subtle as in the second haiku. The word "clean" might resonate with Biblical words and expressions, such as "clear as crystal," "clear as glass," and "nothing unclean shall enter it."[5] The second haiku can be read as Kerouac's depiction of the state of beatitude that can be attained in human life. Another Road haiku, as the following one shows, has a direct reference to a Christian saint and martyr:[6]

O Sebastian, where art thou?
       Pa, watch over us!
Saints, thank you!

                                         (*Book of Haikus* 112)

Whereas Kerouac's vision of the beatific is influenced by Christianity, Dean's is not. Midway on their journey, the two men have a serious discussion on God:

> Dean was tremendously excited about everything he saw, everything he talked about, every detail of every moment that passed. He was out of his mind with real belief. "And of course now, no one can tell us that there is no God. We've passed through all forms. You rembember, Sal, when I first came to New York and I wanted Chad King to teach me about Nietzsche. You see how long ago? Everything is fine, God exists, we know time. Everything since the Greeks has been predicted wrong. You can't make it with geometry and geometrical systems of thinking. It's all *this!*" (*On the Road* 120)

Dean gives an illustration for his observation that God exists: driving on the road, for example, takes place by itself. "As we roll along this way," Dean tells Kerouac, "I am positive beyond doubt that everything will be taken care of for us . . . the thing will go along of itself and you won't go off the road and I can sleep . . ." (*On the Road* 121). Although Kerouac finds it difficult to follow Dean's argument, he is nevertheless persuaded of Dean's observation that God exists.

Toward the end of the journey, Kerouac begins to have a pantheistic vision of the world. Traveling in the Western states with Dean, he finds himself in the midst of an open space at night under a cloudless sky:

> At night in this part of the Wrest the stars, as I had seen them in Wyoming, are big as roman candles and as lonely as the Prince of the Dharma who's lost his ancestral grave and journeys across the spaces between points in the handle of the Big Dipper, trying to find it again. So they slowly wheeled the night, and then long before actual sunrise the great red light appeared far over the dun bleak land toward West Kansas and the birds took up their trill above Denver. (*On the Road* 223)

That Kerouac calls "the Seven Stars," a biblical terminology, "Big Dipper," a cosmological one suggests that he is envisioning the universe as a pantheist.

At the end of the road on their final journey, Kerouac and Dean are elated to see a group of ranchers engaged in their daily activities in a border town in Mexico. They witness the lives of the ranchers protected by God under the bright sky. They came to see human life in harmony with the vast, infinite universe:

> Schooled in the raw road night, Dean was come into the world to see it. He bent over the wheel and looked both ways and rolled along slowly. We stopped for gas the other side of Sabinas Hidalgo. Here a congregation of local straw-hatted

ranchers with handlebar mustaches growled and joked in front of antique gas-
pumps. Across the fields an old man plodded with a burro in front of his switch
stick. The sun rose pure on pure and ancient activities of human life. (*On the
Road* 278)

As Kerouac is creating in his mind beatific images with Biblical expressions,
he is also seeing human life from the perspective of cosmology. At the end
of the journey, Kerouac's effort to envision the beatific state of human life is
intensified not only by his strong faith in Christianity but also by his latent
interest in pantheism.

In the Road haiku Kerouac composed several haiku that depict the infinite,
immutable universe. As the following haiku show, the depiction of the world
conveys the philosophical concepts of cosmology rather than the religious
doctrine of All Mighty:

The microscopic red bugs
        in the sea-side sand
Do they meet and greet?

                                                    (*Book of Haikus* 111)

Hand in hand in a red valley
        with the universal schoolteacher—
the first morning

                                                    (*Book of Haikus* 111)

In the first haiku, focused on the microscopic world, Kerouac is able to
imagine the beatific state of life. In the second haiku, the landscape of the
mountain range is depicted by analogy with human life. Kerouac's vision is
widened in the second haiku as it is narrowed in the first. One cannot physi-
cally see the insect world, nor can one the universe, but one can imagine
such spaces in the universe. Both haiku not only thrive on the depiction of
beatific state of life, but also the images, "red bugs" and "a red valley," are
beautiful to look at. The first haiku features the cordial, friendly relationships of the bugs as the second express the warm, respectful relationships
between teacher and pupil.

In the following haiku Kerouac depicts the immutable state of the universe,
represented by nature on earth:

Who cares about the pop-off trees
        of Provence?—
A road's a road

                                                    (*Book of Haikus* 112)

The backyard I tried to draw
    —It still looks
The same

(Book of Haikus 117)

In the first haiku, as he sees dead trees by the road, Kerouac envisions the state of nature beyond human control. Similarly the second haiku expresses the immutable state of nature. He gives an admonition that humans must abide by the law and order of the universe to attain the beatific state of life for them.

The following haiku by Kerouac also expresses the immutable state of nature and the universe:

Reflected upsidedown
    In the sunset lake, pines
Pointing to infinity

(Book of Haikus 101)

This haiku focuses on an image of the universe that makes human existence infinitesimal in contrast to an infinite space that represents the universe. The image of pines reflected in the lake bears a resemblance to that of "the sacred pin-tree" in Emerson's famous poem, "The Problem":[7]

Or how the sacred pine-tree adds
    To her old leaves new myriads?

Kerouac is impressed, as is Emerson, with the infinity of the universe. Emerson's argument is that divinity, which represents the universe is proven by nature, not by the church or human achievements like huge pyramids in Egypt and ancient temples in Greece. Similarly, Kerouac envisions the scope of the universe by looking at the pines reflected upside down in the sunset lake.[8]

Similarly, Kerouac's haiku, "Dust—the Blizzard," and Emerson's, "The Snow-Storm," both express the Confucian worldview that the universe consists of heaven, earth, and humans:

Dusk—The Blizzard
    Hides everything,
Even the night

(Book of Haikus 38)

Announced by all the trumpets of the sky,
Arrives the snow, and, driving o'er the fields,
Seems nowhere to alight: the whited air

Hides hills and woods, the river, and the heaven,
And veils the farm-house at the garden's end.[9]

(Emerson, "The Snow-Storm")

Both poems depict the supremacy of heaven over the earth and human beings.

The following haiku, "In the Sun," suggests that human law and action must follow the law and order of the universe:

In the sun
        the butterfly wings
Like a church window

(*Book of Haikus* 62)

So does the haiku "THE LIGHT BULB":

THE LIGHT BULB
        SUDDENLY WENT OUT—
STOPPED READING

(*Book of Haikus* 64)

At night, without light from the sun, humans cannot see.

Confucianism, as R. H. Blyth shows, teaches "the sense of something that feeds the life of man, which can be absorbed into our own life and yet have a life of its own, which is organic and growing."[10] Some of Kerouac's haiku convey the Confucian thought that life in whatever form it exists is organic and generative. For example,

Waiting for the leaves
        to fall;—
There goes one!

(*Book of Haikus* 32)

not only illustrates an organic phenomenon, but also captures a moment of change in nature. In the following haiku,

No telegram today
        —Only more
Leaves fell

(*Book of Haikus* 5)

Juxtaposing humanity to nature, Kerouac observes that nature is far more organic and far less isolated than humanity.

In his quest for the beatific in human life, Kerouac is always thinking about sex. From time to time he reflects on the subject, thinking what sex means to him, as well as to others. To Dean, sex represents the physical desire of a male. Kerouac tells Dean, as quoted earlier: "You have absolutely no regard for anybody but yourself and your damned kicks. All you think about is what's hanging between your legs" (*On the Road* 194). *On the Road* begins with the first impression Kerouac had of Dean when they first met in New York. "Dean," remarks Kerouac, "had dispatched the occupant of the apartment to the kitchen, probably to make coffee, while he proceeded with his love-problems, for to him sex was the one and only holy and important thing in life" (*On the Road* 2).

Kerouac, on the other hand, agrees with Dean that sex is holy. But observing Dean's unstable relationships with his wives has convinced Kerouac that Dean's view of sex is the least spiritual. In the first chapter of the novel Kerouac characterizes Dean as if he were an animal:

Dean just raced in society, eager for bread and love; he didn't care one way or the other, "so long's I can get that lil ole gal with that lil sumpin down there tween her legs, boy," and "so long's we can *eat*, son, y'ear me? I'm *hungry*, I'm *starving*, let's *eat right now!*"—and off we'd rush to *eat*, whereof, as saith Ecclesiastes, "It is your portion under the sun." (*On the Road* 8)

To Kerouac, sex is a centerpiece of the beatific state of life. "Somewhere along the line," remarks Kerouac, "I knew there'd be girls, visions, everything; somewhere along the line the pearl would be handed to me" (*On the Road* 8). In his mind, sex is not the physical act itself but, surrounded and protected by "visions, everything," it constitutes a beautiful, precious experience signified by "the pearl."

Early in the novel Kerouac describes the first experience of sex he had with a young girl Dean introduced to him. "She was a nice little girl, simple and true," writes Kerouac," and tremendously frightened of sex. I told her it was beautiful. I wanted to prove this to her. She let me prove it, but I was too impatient and proved nothing" (*On the Road* 57). Reflecting on his sexual relationships with Rita and others, Kerouac remarks:

Boys and girls in America have such a sad time together; sophistication demands that they submit to sex immediately without proper preliminary talk. Not courting talk—real straight talk about souls, for life is holy and every moment is precious. (*On the Road* 58)

At the end of the road in Mexico City, Kerouac continues to view sex as a gift from God in contrast to Dean, who believes that sex is a purely physical experience and something that appears "in a pornographic hasheesh daydream in heaven" (*On the Road* 289).

In the following haiku, Kerouac expresses his observation and belief that sex is holy:

Sex—shaking to breed
          as
Providence permits

(*Book of Haikus* 91)

Kerouac views human sexuality as organic as the first line suggests and divine as the third line points out. This haiku recalls Whiteman's lines in "Song of Myself":

      Urge and urge and urge,
      Always the procreant urge of the world.

Out of the dimness opposite equal advance, always substance and
          increase, always sex,
Always a knit of identity, alsways distinction, alsways a breed of life.[11]

Throughout "Song of Myself" Whitman demonstrates his observation and belief that sex is a divine gift. To him, as well as to Kerouac, sex is a representation of God.

Kerouac's vision of sex is extended to other forms of life. Seeding and cross-pollination make plants and grasses grow. Life in whatever form it exists comes from sex; it is organic and generative. The following haiku illustrates that a phenomenon in nature is organic and generative and that it originates from sex:

May grass
          Nothing much
To do

(*Book of Haikus* 118)

May grass, sprouted from seeds and provided with rain and sun, grows naturally and vigorously.

On the Road was the most popular book Kerouac ever wrote. As an autobiography it thrives on the sentient, passionate self-portrait of an open-minded individual in quest of the truths in mid-twentieth-century American life. As his journey progresses, his vision of the world widens. As a devout Catholic,

Kerouac's spiritual vision is influenced by Christian doctrine, but at the end of the journey it is also influenced by Pantheism. Many of Kerouac's haiku, derived from the observations and ideas conveyed in *On the Road*, succinctly and poignantly express them.

NOTES

1. See Kerouac, *Book of Haikus* 106. Editing this group of haiku, Weinreich places them as "Part IV. 1957: Road Haiku / Summer." She further notes: "Kerouac's pocket notebooks contain haiku entries written in New York City, Tangier, Aix-en-Province, London, New York City again, Berkeley, Mexico, and Orlando. As the notebooks and letters of this period show, Kerouac exhorted himself to write haiku, mindful of the traditional methods" (106).

2. Regina Weinreich's comments about "Road Haiku," *Book of Haikus* 106.

3. See Ann Charters, "Introduction," *On the Road* (New York: Viking, 1958), xxix.

4. Kerouac's description of California as "white like washlines and empty-headed" might mean the Buddhist doctrine of *mu*, the state of nothingness.

5. See New Testament, Revelation 21, Verses 11, 18, and 27, respectively.

6. Saint Sebastian (died c. 288) is said to have been killed during the Roman Emperor Diocletian's persecution of Christians.

7. The lines are quoted from Ralf Waldo Emerson, *Selections from Ralph Waldo Emerson*, ed. Stephen E. Whicher (Boston: Houghton Mifflin, 1960), 418.

8. In *The Dharma Bums*, Kerouac sees human existence as a strange beetle when he climbs Mount Hozomeen: "Standing on my head before bedtime on that rock roof of the moonlight I could indeed see that the earth was truly upsidedown and man a weird vain beetle full of strange ideas walking around upsidedown and boasting, and I could realize that man remembered why this dream of planets and plants and Plantagenets was built out of the primordial essence." See Kerouac, *The Dharma Bums* 238.

9. The lines are quoted from *Selections from Ralf Waldo Emerson*, 414.

10. Blyth, *Haiku* 71.

11. See Walt Whitman, *Complete Poetry and Selected Prose*, ed. James E. Miller, Jr. (Boston: Houghton Mifflin, 1959), 26.

Chapter 9

Kerouac's Haiku and
The Dharma Bums

The Dharma Bums (1958) was intended as a sequence to *On the Road* (1957). Just as is *On the Road*, *The Dharma Bums* is Kerouac's quest in search of the truths in human life. As did *On the Road*, *The Dharma Bums* gave an intimate biographical account of himself. Whereas *On the Road* features Kerouac in contrast to Neal Cassady (1926–1968), his companion for the journey, *The Dharma Bums* portrays his companion, Gary Snyder (1930–), as complementary. In *On the Road* Cassady is a friend as well as a foil like Tom Sawyer in Mark Twain's *Adventures of Huckleberry Finn*. In *The Dharma Bums*, not only is Snyder a friend but he is also a teacher who inspires Kerouac in his studies of Buddhism. For the Beat Generation in America at mid-century Kerouac and Snyder created a mutual admiration society.

Kerouac, living in Berkeley with Ginsberg at the time of the Gallery Six poetry reading, first met Snyder, who was living in a shack nearby. Kerouac was immediately impressed by Snyder and especially with his knowledge of Chinese and Japanese. He saw Snyder living with numerous books, including the famous books by Zen scholar D. T. Suzuki and R. H. Blyth's four volumes of Japanese haiku. He saw Snyder immersed in his studies of Zen Buddhism and in his translation of "Cold Mountain" by Medieval Chinese Zen poet Han Shan. While they were walking, Snyder was not only a delightful companion but appeared a blissful individual: "Japhy had on his fine big boots and his little green Swiss cap with feather, and looked elfin but rugged . . . his eyes shine with joy, he's on his way, his heroes are John Muir and Han Shan and Shih-te and Li Po and John Burroughs and Paul Bunyan and Kropotkin" (*Dharma Bums* 54). Later in their walk with rucksacks on their backs like straggling infantrymen, Kerouc said, "Isn't this a hell of a lot greater than The Place? Getting drunk in there on a fresh Saturday morning like this, all bleary and sick, and here we are by the fresh pure lake walking along in this good air, by God it's a haiku in itself" (*Dharma Bums* 55). Snyder responded: "'Comparisons are odious, Smith,' he sent sailing back to me, quoting Cervantes and making a Zen Buddhist observation to boot. 'It don't make a damn frigging difference whether you're in The Place or hiking up Matterhorn, it's all the same old void, boy'" (*Dharma Bums* 55). By "the same old void" Snyder meant the Zen doctrine of *mu*, the state of nothingness. To Kerouac, Snyder was an epitome of Zen philosophy.

In a later discussion of Zen philosophy with Kerouac, Snyder observed: "The mind is nothing but the world, goddammit. Then Horse Ancestor said 'this mind is Buddha.' He also said 'No mind is Buddha.' Then finally talking about Great Plum his boy, 'The plum is ripe'" (*Dharma Bums* 96). Snyder's definition of Buddha as a mind as well as no mind means that Buddha represents a point of view that excludes human subjectivity. To Snyder, Buddha is *mu*, the void, the emptiness, the state of nothingness, all equated to the state of nature. From that domain human subjectivity is barred for its entry.

Kerouac, on the other hand, considered himself a student of Mahayana Buddhism. What attracted him the most about Buddhism in general was his observation that this religion is buttressed on the doctrine of compassion and mercy and that the doctrine resonates with that of Christianity. Kerouac, however, realized that there is a fundamental difference between the Buddhist doctrine of compassion and mercy and that of Christianity. The Buddhist doctrine is based on Buddhist ontology, in which all living beings, humans and nonhumans, the animate and the inanimate, all have their equal existence in the world. Throughout *The Dharma Bums* Kerouac urges the reader that one must love all living beings. He said, "People have good hearts whether or not they live like Dharma Bums. Compassion is the heart of Buddhism" (*Dharma Bums* 132). Walking in the mountains with Snyder, Kerouac felt himself like Natty Bumppo. This pioneer in Fenimore Cooper's *The Prairie* is enormously sympathetic to Hard Heart, a noble Indian, and hesitant to cut down live trees and destroy nature. Kerouac's and Natty Bumppo's compassion for nonhuman beings is reminiscent of Alice Walker's postmodern novel, *The Color Purple*. Celie, its heroine, feels as if her arm were cut down when she is told to cut down a live tree. It is well known that Alice Walker, who grew up a Christian as did Kerouac but later converted to a Buddhist.

At the outset of his journey Kerouac looked like a pilgrim in progress. He was poised to launch his studies of Buddhism, accompanied by Gary Snyder, a Zen-inspired young poet. Not only did he become knowledgeable about Buddhism by reading Blyth's books on Japanese haiku, but also his constant walking and talking in the fields and mountains with Snyder enriched his understanding and practice of the religion. Although Kerouac and Snyder viewed Buddhism from different perspectives and backgrounds, they ultimately came to agree on the basic principles of Buddhism. Both clearly understood and put into practice Buddhahood and Buddhist ontology.

The primary goal in Kerouac's studies of Buddhism was his achievement of Buddhahood. With Blyth as a guide, Kerouac tried to situate the concept of Buddhahood, what he called "the Buddha nature" in the Buddhist doctrine. "The scale of beings in the Buddhist universe," Blyth observed, "puts man midway. The primitive animistic ideas of Japanese fall in with Buddhist system, and all are united by the theory of transmigration. The result is (or is it the cause?) that our sympathies are widened in both directions."[1] Because humans are placed between the animate and the inanimate, Buddhism teaches its followers to have compassion on the animate as well as on the inanimate. The Buddha nature, buttressed by Buddhist ontology, was what Kerouac tried to achieve. In midway in *The Dharma Bums*, Kerouac asserts:

> "I *know* I'm empty, awake, and that there's no difference between me and any-thing else. In other words it means that I've become the same as everything else. It means I've become a Buddha." Then he says, "I felt great compassion for the trees because we were the same thing; I petted the dogs who didn't argue with me ever. All dogs love God. They're wiser than their masters. I told that to the dogs, too, they listened to me perking up their ears and licking my face. They didn't care one way or the other as long as I was there" (145).

Unlike Snyder, Kerouac was drawn to Mahayana Buddhism, which puts more emphasis on the doctrine of compassion and love. In *Haiku: Eastern Culture*, the first volume of the seminal book on haiku, mentioned earlier, Blyth takes the pains to explain the history of Eastern religions and phi-losophies and especially the hybridization of Buddhism and Confucianism in Japanese Buddhism. Kerouac realized in his studies of Buddhism and haiku that Confucianism, a philosophy, is concerned with the relationship between humans and the universe whereas Buddhism, a religion, is concerned with that between humans and the world.

In the beginning of his study of Buddhism, Kerouac was not concerned about the Buddhist mythology or all the names and national flavors of Bud-dhism, such as the hybridization of Buddhism, Confucianism, and Shintoism in Japanese history. He was deeply impressed with "the first of Sakyamuni's four noble truths, *All life is suffering*. And to an extent interested in the third, *The suppression of suffering can be achieved*, which I didn't quite believe was possible then" (*Dharma Bums* 12). Upon further thoughts he added: "I hadn't yet digested the Lankavatara Scripture which eventually shows you that there's nothing in the world but the mind itself, and therefore all's pos-sible including the suppression of suffering" (*Dharma Bums* 12).

While Kerouac considered himself an optimistic, joyful pilgrim, he was worried about his fellow pilgrim. Midway in their pilgrimage Kerouac was struck one day with Snyder's looking depressed and suffering in his shack. Trying to console Snyder, Kerouac heard him say "I'm depressed and everything you're saying just depresses me further" (*Dharma Bums* 170). But moments later he witnessed Snyder chanting Buddhist prayers in high spirits: "At seven in the morning the sun was out and the butterflies were in the roses by my head and a hummingbird did a jet dive right down at me, whistling, and darted away happily" (*Dharma Bums* 171). Kerouac realized that his perception of Snyder's depression was wrong and that springtime lifted Snyder' spirits : "It was one of the greatest mornings in our lives. There he was standing in the doorway of the shack with a big frying pan in his hand banging on it and chanting 'Buddham saranam gocchami . . . Dhammam saranam gocchami . . . Sangham saranam gocchami' and yelling 'Come on, boy, your pancakes are ready! Come and get it! Bang bang bang" and the orange sun was pouring in through the pines and everything was fine again." Kerouac concluded this episode by saying that Snyder in fact "had contemplated that night and decided I was right about hewing to the good old Dharma" (*Dharma Bums* 171).

After Snyder left for Japan to live in a Zen monastery in Kyoto, Kerouac accomplished his search for Buddahood on Mount Hozomeen as he heard a thunder. All of a sudden he saw "a green and rose rainbow shafted right down into Starvation Ridge not three hundred yards away from my door, like a bolt, like a pillar: it came among steaming clouds and orange sun turmoiling.

What is a rainbow, Lord?
     A hoop
For the lowly."

The rain, as he described, "hooped right into Lightning Creek, rain and snow fell simultaneous, the lake was milkwhite a mile below, it was just too crazy." At dusk he "meditated in the yellow half moon of August. Whenever I heard thunder in the mountains it was like the iron of my mother's love" (*Dharma Bums* 241–42).[2] As he descended Mount Mozomeen, he saw "on the lake rosy reflections of celestial vapor," and said, "God, I love you . . . . I have fallen in love with you, God. Take care of us all, one way or the other" (*Dharma Bums* 244).

Kerouac's achievement of the Buddhahood was strengthened by the two doctrines of Buddhism: Buddhist ontology and *mu*, the Zen concept of the state of nothingness. Blyth shows with classic haiku that the Buddhist ontology buttresses what he calls "the theory of transmigration."[3] Buddhists, unlike Christians, believe that both humans and nonhumans possess the soul and that the soul transmigrates between humans and nonhumans. Buddhists thus believe in reincarnation. Buddhist ontology inspired Kerouac to practice the doctrine of compassion for all living beings. The Buddhist concept of *mu* rid him of egotism. If humans can treat nonhumans as their equals, they are not egotists. Kerouac realized that the Christian concept of righteousness is antithetical to the Buddhist concept of *mu*. He said, "I was very rich now, a super myriad trillionaire in Sampatti transcendental graces, because of good humble karma, maybe because I had pitied the dog and forgiven men. But I knew now that I was a bliss heir, and that the final sin, the worst, is righteousness" (*Dharma Bums* 149).

Brought up a Christian, Kerouac conflated the Buddhist doctrine of compassion with that of Christianity. He was eager to put into practice the admonition he had been given by both religions. At the beginning of *The Dharma Bums*, he ran into a stranger and bum on a freight train he got on in Los Angeles. He immediately took pity on him and said: "How about a little wine to warm you up? Maybe you'd like some bread and cheese with your sardines." Kerouac was reminded of the line in the Diamond Sutra that says: "Practice charity without holding in mind any conceptions about charity, for charity after all is just a word." Although he said, "I was very devout in those days and was practicing my religious devotions almost to perfection," he admitted, "Since then I've become a little hypocritical about my lip-service and a little tired and cynical. Because now I am grown so old and neutral. . . . But then I really believed in the reality of charity and kindness and humility and zeal and neutral tranquility and wisdom and ecstasy" (*Dharma Bums* 4–5). The last word in Kerouac's self-appraisal, "ecstasy," was what he conceived as the Buddhist nirvana. To Kerouac, the achievement of nirvana was a reward for the practice of the Buddhist doctrine of compassion.

Later in a discussion with Kerouac on the Buddhist doctrine of compassion and mercy, Snyder posed a question: "But supposing you're reborn in the lower hells and have hot redhot balls of iron shoved down your throat by devils." Snyder responded: "Life's already shoved an iron foot down my mouth. But I don't think that's anything but a dream cooked up by some hysterical monks who didn't understand Buddha's peace under the Bo Tree or for that matter Christ's peace looking down on the heads of his tormentors and forgiving them." About Christ and on compassion and love, Kerouac said to Snyder, "And after all, a lot of people say he is Maitreya,[4] the Buddha prophesied to appear after Sakyamuni, you know, Maitreya means 'Love' in Sanskrit and all Christ talked about was love" (*Dharma Bums* 202).

The Dharma Bums was dedicated to Han Shan, the legendary Medieval Chinese poet.[5] Kerouac was first introduced to Han Shan by Snyder. From

time to time, whenever they discussed Zen, the discussion was often highlighted by Han Shan's vision of the world. That *The Dharma Bums* opens
with the dedication to Han Shan at the suggestion of Snyder and closes with
a vision of Han Shan suggests that Han Shan's vision was what had inspired
Kerouac to achieve and emulate in his studies of Buddhism. Their dialogue
began as Snyder told Kerouac that Snyder was in the midst of translating Han
Shan's famous poem "Cold Mountain."[6] "Han Shan," Snyder told Kerouac,
"you see was a Chinese scholar who got sick of the big city and the world
and took off to hide in the mountains" (*Dharma Bums* 20). Kerouac wondered
why Han Shan was Synder's hero. Snyder said, "Because . . . he was a poet,
a mountain man, a Buddhist dedicated to the principle of meditation on the
essence of all things, a vegetarian too by the way though I haven't got on that
kick from figuring maybe in this modern world to be a vegetarian is to split
hairs a little since all sentient beings eat what they can. And he was a man of
solitude who could take off by himself and live purely and true to himself"
(*Dharma Bums* 22). Later in the book Snyder read to Kerouac Snyder's translation of the key stanza of "Cold Mountain." The last six lines ("I've got no
use for the kulak / With his big barn and pasture— / He just sets up a prison
for himself. / Once in he can't get out. / Think it over— / You know it might
happen to you")[7] is reminiscent of Thoreau's satire in *Walden* on a rich farm-
er's desire to own a mansion that would ironically imprison its owner in it.

Kerouac and Snyder were both struck, on the one hand, with Han Shan's
dedication to the discipline of meditation on the cold mountain and with the
vision he attained by meditation, on the other. When they went out camping
one day, Snyder showed Kerouac the manner of *Zazen* [kneeling] meditation.
As Kerouac spread out his sleeping bag and took off his shoes, sighing happily, slipping his stockinged feet into his sleeping bag, and "looking around
gladly at the beautiful fall trees thinking 'Ah what a night of true sweet
sleep this will be, what meditations I can get into in this intense silence of
Nowhere'" (*Dharma Bums* 47–48). While Snyder was in search of Buddhist
nirvana through *Zazen* meditation, Kerouac was determined to reach the state
of nothingness, nowhere, and silence. While Snyder often concentrated on
chanting of Gocham, the Buddhist prayer of *mu*, nothingness, Snyder tried
to attain *mu* through silence. "I knew," Kerouac told himself "that the sound
of silence was everywhere and therefore everything everywhere was silence"
(*Dharma Bums* 199).

Kerouac was trying to demonstrate that everything on earth, including
himself, is empty and awake. He further argued that there is no difference
between him and anything else on earth. This concept was based on the
concept of *mu*, as well as Buddhist ontology, in which all living beings
have equal existence on earth. What is happening in them, whether in the

animate or the inanimate, have nothing to do with human thoughts and actions. These living beings, representing *mu*, are autonomous and beyond human control, human subjectivity. Kerouac came to envision that everything on earth was nothing, empty: "I am emptiness, I am not different from emptiness, neither is emptiness different from me; indeed, emptiness is me." Once he was able to envision the state of nothingness through meditations, he said, "I almost heard the words said: 'Everything is all right forever and forever and forever.' . . . I felt like yelling it to the stars. I clasped my hands and prayed, 'O wise and serene spirit of Awakenhood, everything's all right forever and forever and forever and thank you thank you thank you amen'" (*Dharma Bums* 137).

Ever since the very beginning of his journey, when he encountered on a freight train in California the little old bum with a slip of paper which contained Saint Teresa's prayer, Kerouac has been obsessed with the infinitesimal human existence on earth. While lying on the beach at night he contemplated the infinity of the universe by wondering how many grains of sand on the beach as there are stars in the sky. Extending his speculation to human existence, he wondered, "How many human beings have there been, in fact how many living creatures have there been, since before the *less* part of beginningless time? Why, oy, I reckon you would have to calculate the number of grains of sand on this beach and on every star in the sky, in every one of the ten thousand great chilicosms, which would be a number of sand grains uncomputable by IBM and Burroughs too, why boy I don't rightly know" (*Dharma Bums* 8). Kerouac's speculation of infinity in the universe is reminiscent of Huck and Jim's speculation in *Adventures of Huckleberry Finn* on how the countless stars came into being.[8] Kerouac, as are Huck and Jim, was convinced of the infinitesimal, negligible existence of human beings. Pitted against the infinity of the universe, the existence of human subjectivity is erased.

Kerouac and Snyder both came to share the same vision of human existence, the Zen concept of the state of nothingness. Shortly before Snyder left for Japan to study Zen, Kerouac, before attaining the final vision of the world, even wondered how human beings' ancestors, the Neanderthal, viewed the world. Kerouac posed a rhetorical question, "Can't you just see all those enlightened monkey men sitting around a roaring woodfire around their Buddha saying nothing and knowing everything?" "The stars," Snyder responded, "were the same then as they are tonight" (*Dharma Bums* 214). Both were in agreement that the world had not changed since time immemorial and that the state of nature was permanent.[9]

At the end of his journey Kerouac witnessed that the void, the hole in the ground, never changed. The truth of nature in this world remained the same. As did Thoreau in *Walden*, Kerouac realized that while the world never

changed, he had changed: he thought he had achieved Buddhist enlightenment. "Morning," he said, "the definite feel of autumn coming, the end of
my job coming, wild windy cloud-crazed days now, a definite golden look in
the high noon haze. Night, made hot cocoa and sang by the woodfire. I called
Han Shan in the mountains: there was no answer. I called Han Shan in the
morning fog: silence, it said. I called: Dipankara[10] instructed me by saying
nothing. Mists blew by, I closed my eyes, the stove did the talking. "Woo!"
I yelled, and the bird of perfect balance on the fir point just moved his tail;
then he was gone and distance grew immensely white" (*Dharma Bums* 242).

The Dharma Bums, like *On the Road*, can be read as a quest taken by
Kerouac in search of individual freedom, an idealism that buttresses the
American dream. The Zen concept of mu Kerouac acquired in his study and
practice of Buddhism yielded his concept of individual freedom. Midway in
his journey, lying on his bag smoking, he thought, "Everything is possible. I
am God, I am Buddha, I am imperfect Ray Smith, all at the same time, I am
empty space, I am all things. I have all the time in the world from life to life
to do what is to do, to do what is done, to do the timeless doing, infinitely
perfect within, why cry, why worry, perfect like mind essence and the minds
of banana peels" (*Dharma Bums* 122). He was at the same time laughing and
remembering his poetic Zen Lunatic Dharma Bum friends of San Francisco
whom he was dearly missing. On another occasion he was sitting in his
Buddha-arbor, colyalcolor "wall of flowers pink and red and ivory white,
among aviaries of magic transcendent birds recognizing my awakening mind
with sweet weird cries (the pathless lark), in the ethereal perfume, mysteri-
ously ancient, the bliss of the Buddha-fields." He then saw that "my life was
a vast glowing empty page and I could do anything I wanted" (*Dharma Bums*
147–48).

Kerouac was eager to know how others in America viewed the idea and
execution of individual freedom. As he was hitchhiking in Arizona he was
picked up by a truck driver from Ohio. He was curious to know if such a
man had individual freedom. The truck driver was equally curious about
Kerouac's Buddhist concept and practice. He asked laughing, "Where'd you
learn to do all these funny things? . . . And you know I say funny but there's
sumptin so durned sensible about 'em. Here I am killin myself drivin this
rig back and forth from Ohio to L.A. and I make more money than you ever
had in your whole life as a hobo, but you're the one who enjoys life and not
only that but you do it without workin or a whole lot of money. Now who's
smart, you or me?" Such comments intimate not only that the truck driver
understood Kerouac's worldview but that he did not have individual freedom.
Kerouac thought that the truck driver "had a nice home in Ohio with wife,
daughter, Christmas tree, two cars, garage, lawn, lawnmower, but he couldn't
enjoy any of it because he really wasn't free." "It was sadly true," he thought.

"I didn't mean I was a better man than he was, however, he was a great man and I liked him and he liked me" (*Dharma Bums* 129) It sounds as though a mutual admiration society was formed by the two men like Kerouac and Snyder. Kerouac was struck not only with the truck driver's self-awareness but also with his ability to understand others.

Although Kerouac found an audience for his Buddhist vision and lifestyle, he found it difficult to persuade his relatives and especially his mother on the principle and practice of Buddhism. On homecoming to visit his mother and relatives living in the pastoral countryside in North Carolina, he imagined his mother was worried he would not make it and thinking, "Poor Raymond, why does he always have to hitchhike and worry me to death, why isn't he like other men?" Upon arrival as he stood in the cold yard looking at her, he thought of Snyder, who hated white tiled sinks and what he called "kitchen machinery," the modern conveniences his mother was living with. To defend her lifestyle he said, "People have good hearts whether or not they live like Dharma Bums" (*Dharma Bums* 132).

Despite her son's strange lifestyle, she witnessed Kerouac's passionate devotion to the Buddhist principle and practice. She saw him spending "all that winter and spring meditating under the trees and finding out by myself the truth of all things. I was very happy." "After they'd gone to bed," Kerouac said, "I put on my jacket and my earmuff cap and railroad gloves and over all that my nylon poncho and strode out in the cotton field moonlight like a shroudy monk" (*Dharma Bums* 132–33). On another night he meditated accompanied by dogs. "The dogs," he saw, "meditated on their paws. We were all absolutely quiet. The entire moony countryside was frosty silent, not even the little tick of rabbits or coons anywhere. An absolute cold blessed silence." Silence then led to the state of nothingness. "A blessed night," he said. "I immediately fell into a blank thoughtless trance wherein it was again revealed to me 'This thinking has stopped' and I sighed because I didn't have to think any more and felt my whole body sink into a blessedness surely to be believed, completely relaxed and at peace with all the ephemeral world of dream and dreamer and the dreaming itself" (*Dharma Bums* 134).

"After a while," Kerouac realized, "my meditations and studies began to bear fruit." One cold night in the woods in absolute silence it seemed that he heard the words saying: "Everything is all right forever and forever and forever." He repeated his prayer, "O wise and serene spirit of Awakenerhood, everything's all right forever and forever and forever and thank you thank you thank you amen." Praying with the words "Awakenerhood" and "amen" suggests that Kerouac was indeed conflating Buddhism and Christianity in his search for the truths of life. He often referred to Gautama Buddha's enlightenment under the Bo Tree as well as Christ's sacrifice on the Cross. Contemplating death and eternity, he said, "I realized that this was the truth

Rosie knew now, and all the dead, my dead father and dead brother and dead uncles and cousins and aunts, the truth that is realizable in a dead man's bones and is beyond the Tree of Buddha as well as the Cross of Jesus. *Believe* that the world is an ethereal flower, and ye live" (*Dharma Bums* 137). Kerouac's argument is that the truth of life lies beyond Buddha's enlightenment and Christ's death. For Kerouac, the truth of life means the Zen concept of the state of nothingness and the state of nothingness is his nirvana.

As he was going around the country as a Buddhist bum, he was also traveling as if he were a roaming bard like Basho. Meditations in the fields and woods and studies of Buddhism at home and in the library led to his composing numerous haiku in his mind. He often talked with Gary Snyder with the theory and technique of haiku composition. As mentioned in *The Dharma Bums*, Kerouac, while reading a number of books on Buddhism, also consulted the four volume book on Japanese haiku by R. H. Blyth, especially the first volume, subtitled "Eastern Culture." "Kerouac's pocket notebooks," as Regina Weinreich notes, contained "haiku entries written in New York City, Tangier, Aix-en-Provence, London, New York City again, Berkeley, Mexico, and Orlando. As the notebooks and letters of this period show, Kerouac exhorted himself to write haiku, mindful of the traditional methods" (*Book of Haikus* 106).

Kerouac, while hiking in the mountains with Snyder, said: "Walking in this country you could understand the perfect gems of haikus the Oriental poets had written, never getting drunk in the mountains or anything but just going along as fresh as children writing down what they saw without literary devices of fanciness of expression. We made up haikus as we climbed, winding up and up now on the slopes of brush" (*Dhama Bums* 59). Snyder responded: "A real haiku's gotta be as simple as porridge and yet make you see the real thing, like the greatest haiku of them all probably is the one that goes 'The sparrow hops along the veranda, with wet feet.' By Shiki. You see the wet footprints like a vision in your mind and yet in those few words you also see all the rain that's been falling that day and almost smell the wet pine needles'" (*Dharma Bums* 59).

Kerouac and Snyder both emphasized that haiku must be simple, the principle that Blyth considers a salient characteristic of haiku. As an example Blyth quotes a haiku Basho composed on his travels, as mentioned earlier:

> The Rose of Sharon
> By the roadside,
>   Was eaten by the horse.[11]

"What Bashō means," Blyth remarks, "is something that belongs to Zen, namely, that we must not wish to do something clever, write a fine poem, but do it as naturally, as freely, as unselfconsciously as a child does everything."[12] Blyth further quotes another haiku by Basho and a haiku by Issa to illustrate the simplicity of haiku:[13]

You light the fire;
I'll show you something nice,—
        A great ball of snow!

(Basho)

I could eat it!—
This snow that falls
        So softly, so softly.

(Issa)

Both haiku are depictions of simple, natural phenomena in nature but Basho's haiku expresses some subjectivity of aesthetics as does Issa's more subjectivity of desire.

Following the principle of simplicity and naturalness, Kerouac wrote numerous haiku such as:

Chipmunk went in
—butterfly
Came out

(*Book of Haikus* 95)

Sunday—
        The sky is blue,
The flowers are red

(*Book of Haikus* 103)

The little white cat
        Walks in the grass
With his tail up in the air

(*Book of Haikus* 115)

Birds chirp
        fog
Bugs the gate

(*Book of Haikus* 122)

April mist—
        under the pine
At midnight

(*Book of Haikus* 123)

Wet fog
    shining
In lamplit leaves

                                            (*Book of Haikus* 124)

Mist falling
    —Purple flowers
Growing

                                            (*Book of Haikus* 125)

The wind sent
    A leaf on
The robin's back

                                            (*Book of Haikus* 175)

The following haiku by Kerouac in depicting natural phenomena in nature contains images of humanity:

Late afternoon—
    the lakes sparkle
Blinds me

                                            (*Book of Haikus* 102)

I made raspberry fruit jello
    The color of rubies
In the setting sun

                                            (*Book of Haikus* 102)

Loves his own belly
    The way I love my life,
The white cat

                                            (*Book of Haikus* 115)

The moon is moving,
    thru the clouds
Like a slow balloon

                                            (*Book of Haikus* 171)

A bird hanging
    on the wire
At dawn

                                            (*Book of Haikus* 173)

In the first three haiku, "Late Afternoon—," "I Made Raspberry Fruit Jello," and "Loves His Own Belly," while depicting natural phenomena in nature, Kerouac is self-conscious. Like Basho's and Issa's haiku quoted above, these haiku by Kerouac subtly express subjectivity. The last two haiku, "The Moon Is Moving" and "A Bird Hanging," though they are simple, natural depictions of nature, include images of humanity, "a slow balloon" and "the wire," that depict human made objects, and indirectly express subjectivity. In "The Moon Is Moving," Kerouac might be surprised by the slow, leisurely pace the moon is moving; in "A Bird Hanging," he might be struck with a bird hanging on the wire rather than on a branch of a tree.

Kerouac grew up a Christian but as he acquired the Buddhahood trough his study and meditation he began to conflate Christian and Buddhist doctrines. But he learned that Mahayana Buddhism puts more emphasis on compassion and love than does Confucianism. For Kerouac, the doctrine that all things in the universe have the Buddha nature distinguishes Buddhism from Confucianism, as well as from Christianity. The concept of Buddhahood thus inspired him to love and have compassion for all things, the inanimate and the inanimate, the human and the subhuman.[14] In several of his haiku, he directly expressed his achievement of Buddhahood:

I close my eyes—
        I hear & see
Mandala

                                        (*Book of Haikus* 85)

"I Close My Eyes" envisions the self in an image of Mandala, a Buddhist divinity. Another piece on Buddha,

The mountains
        are mighty patient,
Buddha-man

                                        (*Book of Haikus* 86)

depicts an image of Buddha in terms of nature rather than a figure. In the following piece,

While meditating
        I am Buddha—
Who else?

                                        (*Book of Haikus* 97)

Buddha is defined as a concept; a meditation yields such a concept. Kerouac is illustrating the Buddhist enlightenment by which to reach a state of mind in which one has effaced subjectivity and attained satori.

From time to time Kerouac indirectly portrays in his haiku the attainment of satori, for instance:

Quietly pouring coffee
          in the afternoon,
How pleasant!

                                                        (*Book of Haikus* 47)

Such a haiku expresses comfort and peace of mind that derive from the tranquillity of one's environment. The haiku "Hot Coffee" conveys a similar sentiment:

Hot coffee
          and a cigarette—
Why zazen?

                                                        (*Book of Haikus* 88)

In contrast to the previous haiku, this one can be read as an argument against drinking coffee and smoking. Kerouac wondered if drinking coffee and smoking a cigarette might prevent the mind from attaining satori. He thus questioned why *zazen*, a practice of Zen, would result in the attainment of satori. The argument against drinking and smoking is reminiscent of Thoreau's admonition against such activities.[15]

Kerouac's love and compassion was extended to nonhuman beings, as shown in some of his best haiku:

In my medicine cabinet
          the winter fly
Has died of old age

                                                        (*Book of Haikus* 12)

A bird on
          the branch out there
—I waved

                                                        (*Book of Haikus* 33)

In the first piece, "In My Medicine Cabinet," humanity is pitted against nature. It is ironic that as medicine helps humans, it does not help flies. Not only does this haiku express sympathy for the death of a fly people would not like to see in their home, it suggests that the fly would have died peacefully outdoors. "A Bird on," on the other hand, not only expresses the feeling of love and friendship a person has for a bird, but also captures a moment of affinity between the two living beings, the unity of humanity and nature.

In the following haiku, Kerouac demonstrates the Buddhist doctrine of mercy and compassion in contrast to Christianity:

Woke up groaning
        with a dream of a priest
Eating chicken necks

                                                        (*Book of Haikus* 31)

betrays a nightmare a Christian converted Buddhist like Kerouac would have. This haiku suggests Kerouac's view of Christians' cruelty to animals in contrast to Buddhists' belief in the existence of soul in animals.

Not only was Kerouac influenced by Mahayana Buddhism, especially its doctrine of Buddhahood and mercy, he also became interested in Zen Buddhism as he discussed its philosophy and practice with Gary Snyder, who studied Zen in Japanese monasteries. What distinguishes Zen from the rest of the sects is Zen's emphasis on the state of mind called "mu," nothingness. In *Nozarashi Kiko* (*A Travel Account of My Exposure in the Fields*), Basho, a Zen Buddhist, wrote: "When I set out on my journey of a thousand leagues I packed no provisions for the road. I clung to the staff of that pilgrim of old who, it is said, 'entered the realm of nothingness under the moon after midnight.'"[16] Several of Kerouac's haiku depict the state of nothingness:

Everywhere beyond
        the Truth,
Empty space blue

                                                        (*Book of Haikus* 86)

"Everywhere Beyond," is reminiscent of the empty space the whiteness of the whale symbolizes in Melville's *Moby-Dick*.[17] Another piece on the Zen state of mind,

Spring day–
        in my mind
Nothing

                                                        (*Book of Haikus* 124)

bears a resemblance to Richard Wright's haiku:

It is September,
The month in which I was born;
    And I have no thoughts.

                                        (Wright, Haiku 127)

To enter the state of nothingness, one must annihilate oneself. The undisciplined self is often misguided by egotism. In Zen, one's self-reliance precludes the attainment of satori, because one's consciousness of self means that one is not completely free of one's thoughts and feelings and has not identified self with the absolute. Whereas Mahayana Buddhism, as practiced in the Jodo sect in Japan, in which one can achieve one's salvation by praying to the Buddha, Zen Buddhism, as practiced in the Rinzai sect, urges its followers even to "kill the Buddha" to attain their enlightenment. Some of Kerouac's haiku convey Rinzai's admonition:

There's no Buddha
        because
There's no me

                                        (*Book of Haikus* 75)

I called Hanshan
        in the mountains
—there was no answer

                                        (*Book of Haikus* 93)

All these haiku express the Zen discipline of mind that the ultimate truth lies not in self or another person, or even a divine figure such as Buddha and Christ. The ultimate truth emerges in the state of nothingness—nature itself. Shiki expressed a similar point of view in this haiku:

The wind in autumn
As for me, there are no gods,
There are no Buddhas.[18]

                                        (Shiki)

As the following haiku by Kerouac show, effacing the subject, the suppression of egotism, is expressed indirectly:

The trees are putting on
        Noh plays—
Booming, roaring

                                        (*Book of Haikus* 125)

"The Trees Are Putting On" is a portrayal of nature that has nothing to do with the subject who is watching the trees. At the same time the trees are likened to *noh* plays, which enact the Zen doctrine that one must suppress egotism and subjectivity. Another piece on the Zen discipline of mind,

The train speeding
        thru emptiness
—I was a trainman

(*Book of Haikus* 125)

describes the subject, a train speeding through emptiness, a space that constitutes the realm of nothingness. The subject, which is infinitesimal and is pitted against a vast space, cannot claim its place in it. Another haiku on the absence of human subjectivity,

Lay the pencil
        away—no more
thoughts, no lead

(*Book of Haikus* 139)

concerns the state of nothingness, where human thoughts cannot enter.

Still some other haiku intimate that human subjectivity is irrelevant and suspect:

I said a joke
        under the stars
—No laughter

(*Book of Haikus* 39)

You'd be surprised
        how little I knew
Even up to yesterday

(*Book of Haikus* 65)

These pieces all illustrate the human mind, subjectivity, is negligible as opposed to nature, objectivity. The second haiku, "You'd Be Surprised," suggests that knowledge originates in nature. In the following haiku,

Take up a cup of water
        from the ocean
And there I am

(*Book of Haikus* 66)

Kerouac tries to prove how small and irrelevant an individual is in the midst of an ocean. Another haiku on the same subject,

Or, walking the same or different
        paths
The moon follows each

(Book of Haikus 66)

not only demonstrates the primacy of nature over humanity, but describes how human action is dictated by universal law: as human existence is ephemeral as nature is ubiquitous.

As a Beat writer, Kerouac was inspired by the Zen doctrine that to attain enlightenment is to reach the state of nothingness. Not only is this state of mind free of human subjectivity and egotism, it is even free of religious conception. The Rinzai Zen, as noted earlier, teaches its followers that if they see Buddha in their meditations, they must "kill" him. At the same time, Kerouac was deeply influenced by Mahayana Buddhism which teaches that one can achieve Buddhahood in life or death and that the human soul, buttressed by the virtues of mercy and compassion, transmigrate from one living being to another.

In *The Dharma Bums*, Gary Snyder, a Zen Buddhist, had a series of dialogue with Kerouac, a Mahayana Buddhist, that revealed the two different religiosities the two branches of Buddhism represented. Before Kerouac was immersed in his study and practice of Buddhism, he was well versed in the writings of American transcendentalists, such as Emerson, Thoreau, and Whitman. He also found American transcendentalists well acquainted with Confucianism and Buddhism. Through interactions with his fellow Beats, Allen Ginsberg and Gary Snyder, as *The Dharma Bums* describes, as well as through his studies of Buddhism, Zen, and R. H. Blyth's *Haiku: Eastern Culture*, in particular, he firmly established his poetics. The numerous haiku he wrote reflect his study and practice of Buddhism as a religion as well as a philosophy. What is remarkable about his haiku is that not only was he influenced by the books he studied, but he was also inspired by his own experiences in wandering and meditating in the fields and on the mountains in America.

NOTES

1. Blyth, *Haiku* 19.
2. Evoking his mother in his meditation has an affinity to Whitman's allusion to the old mother in "Out of the Cradle Endlessly Rocking":

The aria sinking,
All else continuing, the stars shining,
The winds blowing, the notes of the bird continuous echoing,
With angry moans the fierce old mother incessantly moaning,

(*Complete Poetry* 183)

    3. Blyth, *Haiku* 19.

    4. Maitreya is regarded as a future Buddha of this world in Buddhist eschatology. In some Buddhist literature, such as the Amitabba Sutra and the Lotus Sutra, a Buddist text Kerouac often cites, Maitreya is referred to as Ajita Budhisattva. Maitreya is a bodhisattra who in the Buddhist tradition is to appear on Earth, achieve complete enlightenment, and teach the pure dharma.

    5. Han Shan, in Chinese characters寒山 (Cold Mountain), was a legendary and often fabled Chinese poet in the ninth century. His poems were translated into English by Authur Waley (1954), whom Kerouac mentions in *The Dharma Bums*, and Gary Snyder (1958), and Burton Watson (1970).

    6. The following is Synder's translation of "Cold Mountain," published in 1958, the same year *The Dharma Bums* appeared:

Cold Mountain is a house
Without beams or walls.
The six doors left and right are open
The hall is blue sky.
The rooms all vacant and vague
The east wall beats on the west wall
At the center nothing.

Borrowers don't bother me
In the cold I build a little fire
When I'm hungry I boil up some greens.
I've got no use for the kulak
With his big barn and pasture—
He just sets up a prison for himself.
Once in he can't get out.
Think it over—
You know it might happen to you.

(*Anthology of American Literature II*: 1687)

    7. The entire stanza of "Cold Mountain" is in note 6.

    8. Lying on a raft in the Mississippi, Huck says, "It's lovely on live on a raft. We had the sky, up there, all speckled with stars, and we used to lay on our backs and look up at them, and discuss about whether they was made, or only just happened—Jim he allowed they was made, but I allowed they happened; I judged it would have took too long to *make* so many. Jim said the moon could a *laid* them; well, that looked kind of reasonable, so I didn't say nothing against it, because I've seen a frog lay most as many, so of course it could be done. We used to watch the stars that fell, too, and see them streak down. Jim allowed they'd got spoiled and was hove out of the nest" (*Adventures of Huckleberry Finn* (New York: Norton), 97).

9. When Thoreau returned to Walden Pond, he saw that while the pond had stayed the same, he had changed. Living in the woods by Walden Pond changed his worldview.

10. Theoretically, the number of Buddhas having existed is enormous and they are often collectively known by the name of "Thousand Buddhas." Each was responsible for a life cycle. According to some Buddhist traditions, Dipankara was a Buddha who reached enlightenment eons prior to Gautama, the historical Buddha.

11. Blyth, *Haiku* 217.

12. Ibid.

13. Ibid. The translation of Basho's and Issa's haiku is by Blyth.

14. In *The Dharma Bums*, as Kerouac hitchhiked home to see his mother in North Carolina, he thought of her and Gary Snyder. Kerouac wrote about Snyder: "Why is he so mad about white tiled sinks and 'kitchen machinery' he calls it?" Referring to his mother's doing the dishes in the white sink, Kerouac remarked, "People have good hearts whether or not they live like Dharma Bums. Compassion is the heart of Buddhism" (105). At the end of his journey to Mount Hozomeen, Kerouac witnessed "the world was upsidedown hanging in an ocean of endless space and here were all these people sitting in theaters watching movies . . . . Pacing in the yard at dusk, singing 'Wee Small Hours,' when I came to the lines 'when the whole wide world is fast asleep' my eyes filled with tears, 'Okay world,' I said, 'I'll love ya.' In bed at night, warm and happy in my bag on the good hemp bunk, I'd see my table and my clothes in the moonlight . . . and on this I'd go to sleep like a lamb" (187–88).

15. *Walden* teaches the virtue of drinking pure water, for drinking tea, coffee, wine, or smoking tobacco, opium, and so on. would harm not only one's physical health but one's mental health: "I believe that water is the only drink for a wise man; wine is not so noble a liquor; and think of dashing the hopes of a morning with a cup of warm coffee, or of an evening with a dish of tea! Ah, how low I fall when I am tempted by them!" (217).

16. Donald Keene, *World within Walls: Japanese Literature of the Pre-Modern Era, 1600–1868* (New York: Grove, 1976), 81.

17. Melville writes: "Is it that by its indefiniteness it shadows forth the heartless voids and immensities of the universe, and thus stabs us from behind with the thought of annihilation, when beholding the white depths of the milky way? Or is it, that as in essence whiteness is not so much a color as the visible absence of color, and at the same time the concrete of all colors; is it for these reasons that there is such a dumb blankness, full of meaning, in a wide landscape of snows—a colorless, all-color of atheism from which we shrink?" (169).

18. The translation of Shiki's haiku is by Hakutani.

Part II

SELECTED HAIKU BY
JACK KEROUAC

List of Kerouac's Haiku
from *Book of Haikus*

A big fat flake
      of snow
Falling all alone

(54)

A bird hanging
      on the wire
At dawn

(173)

A bird on
      the branch out there
—I waved

(33)

A bottle of wine,
      a bishop—
Everything is God

(108)

A quiet Autumn night
      and these fools
Are starting to argue

(177)

After the shower,
      among the drenched roses,
The bird thrashing in the bath

(14)

Ah, the crickets
        are screaming
at the moon

(140)

All these sages
        Sleep
With their mouths open

(117)

Am I a flower
        bee, that you
Stare at me?

(155)

April mist—
        Under the pine
At midnight

(123)

Bee, why are you
        staring at me?
I'm not a flower!

(15)

Birds chirp
        Fog
Bugs the gate

(122)

Content, the top trees
        shrouded
In gray fog

(85)

Dawn—crows cawing
        ducks quack quacking,
Kitchen windows lighting

(50)

Desk cluttered
        with mail—
My mind is quiet

(145)

Desolation, Desolation,
     so hard
To come down off of

                         (98)

Dusk—The Blizzard
     Hides everything,
Even the night

                         (38)

Everywhere beyond
     the Truth
Empty space blue

                         (86)

Following each other,
     my cats stop
when it thunders

                         (27)

Frozen
     in the birdbath,
A leaf

                         (5)

Glow worms
     brightly sleeping
On my flowers

                         (137)

Greyhound bus,
     flowing all night,
Virginia

                         (114)

Hand in hand in a red valley
     With the universal school teacher—
the first morning

                         (111)

High noon
     in Northport
—Alien shore

                         (137)

Hot coffee
      and a cigarette—
Why zazen?

           (88)

I close my eyes—
      I hear & see
Mandala

           (85)

I called—Dipankara
      instructed me
By saying nothing

           (93)

I called Hanshan
      in the mountains
—there was no answer

           (93)

I made raspberry fruit jello
      The color of rubies
In the setting sun

           (102)

I said a joke
      under the stars
—No laughter

           (39)

Ignoring my bread,
      the bird peeking
In the grass

           (24)

In back of the Supermarket
      In the parking lot weeds
Purple flowers

           (18)

In enormous blizzard
      burying everything
My cat's out making

           (164)

In my medicine cabinet
      the winter fly
Has died of old age

                                     (12)

In the sun
      the butterfly wings
Like a church window

                                     (62)

Jack reads his book
      aloud at night
—the stars come out.

                                   (133)

Late afternoon—
      the lakes sparkle
Blinds me

                                   (102)

Lay the pencil
      away—no more
thoughts, no lead

                                   (139)

Loves his own belly
      The way I love my life,
The white cat

                                   (115)

Looking for my cat
      in the weeds,
I found a butterfly

                                   (40)

May grass—
      Nothing much
To do

                                   (118)

Mist falling
      —Purple flowers
Growing

                                   (125)

No telegram today
        —Only more
Leaves fell

                                                    (5)

O Sebastian, where are thou?
        Pa, watch over us!
Saints, thank you!

                                                    (112)

On Desolation
        I was the alonest man
in the world

                                                    (136)

Or, walking the same or different
        paths
The moon follows each

                                                    (66)

Perfect moonlit night—
        marred
By family squabbles

                                                    (17)

Quietly pouring coffee
        in the afternoon,
How pleasant!

                                                    (47)

Rainy night,
        the top leaves wave
In my gray sky

                                                    (64)

Reading the sutra
        I decided
To go straight

                                                    (143)

Reflected upsidedown
        In the sunset lake, pines
Pointing to infinity

                                                    (101)

Rig rig rig—
      that's the rat
On the roof

                                                  (92)

River wonderland—
      The emptiness
Of the golden eternity

                                               (100)

Sex—shaking to breed
      as
Providence permits

                                               (91)

Shall I break God's commandment?
      Little fly
Rubbing its back legs

                                             (109)

Shall I heed God's commandment?
      —wave breaking
On the rocks—

                                             (109)

Shall I say no?
      —fly rubbing
its back legs

                                             (78)

Shooting star!—no,
      lightning bug!—
ah well, June night

                                             (151)

Spring day—
      In my mind
Nothing

                                             (124)

Spring evening—
      hobo with hard on
Like bamboo

                                             (144)

Sunday—
    the sky is blue,
The flowers are red

                                           (103)

Take up a cup of water
    from the ocean
And there I am

                                           (66)

The Angel's hair
    trailed on my chin
Like a cobweb

                                         (138)

The backyard I tried to draw
    —it still looks
The same

                                         (117)

The crickets—crying
    for rain—
Again?

                                         (23)

The bottom of my shoes
    are clean
From walking in the rain

                                         (8)

The cows of Autumn—
    laughing along the fence,
Roosters at Dawn

                                         (174)

The droopy constellation
    on the grassy hill—
Emily Dickinson's Tomb

                                         (154)

The jazz trombone,
    The moving curtain,
—Spring rain

                                         (114)

THE LIGHT BULB
    SUDDENLY WENT OUT—
STOPPED READING

                                                         (64)

The little white cat
    Walks in the grass
With his tail up in the air

                                                       (115)

The microscopic red bugs
    in the sea-side sand
Do they meet and greet?

                                                       (111)

The moon is moving,
    thru the clouds
Like a slow balloon

                                                       (171)

The mountains
    are mighty patient,
Buddha-man

                                                       (86)

The rose moves
    Like a Reichian disciple
On its stem

                                                       (121)

The summer chair
    rocking by itself
In the blizzard

                                                       (36)

The train speeding
    thru emptiness
—I was a train man

                                                       (125)

The tree looks
    like a dog
Barking at Heaven

                                                       (3)

The trees are putting on
      Noh plays—
Booming, roaring

                                                  (125)

The vigorous bell-ringing priest
      the catch in the harbor

                                                  (110)

The wind sent
      a leaf on
The robin's back

                                                  (175)

There is no deep
      Turning-about
in the Void

                                                  (75)

There's no Buddha
      because
There's no me

                                                  (75)

There's nothing there
      because
I dont care

                                                  (87)

This July evening,
      A large frog
On my doorsill

                                                  (18)

Waiting for the leaves
      to fall;—
There goes one!

                                                  (32)

Wet fog
      shining
In lamplit leaves

                                                  (124)

What is a rainbow, Lord?
    A hoop
For the lowly.

                                      (*Dharma Bums* 241)

While meditating
    I am Buddha—
Who else?

                                      (97)

Who cares about the pop-off trees
    Of Provence?—
A road's a road

                                      (112)

Woke up groaning
    with a dream of a priest
Eating chicken necks

                                      (31)

You'd be surprised
    How little I knew
Even up to yesterday

                                      (65)

Work Cited

Akimoto, Fujio. *Haiku Nyumon*. Tokyo: Kodansha, 1971.

Aldington, Richard. "Penultimate Poetry." *Egoist* (15 January 1915).

Blyth, R. H. *Haiku*. 4 vols. Tokyo: Hokuseido, 1949.

———. *A History of Haiku*. 2 vols. Tokyo: Hokuseido, 1963, 1964.

———. *Haiku: Eastern Culture*. Tokyo: Hokuseido, 1981.

Brooks, Gwendolyn. *Selected Poems*. New York: Harper Perennial, 1963, 1999.

Carpenter, Humphrey. *A Serious Character: The Life of Ezra Pound*. Boston: Houghton Mifflin, 1988.

Cather, Willa. "Two Poets: Yone Noguchi and Bliss Carman." In *The World and the Parish: Willa Cather's Articles and Reviews, 1893–1902*. Edited by William M. Martin. Lincoln: University of Nebraska Press, 1970.

Charters, Ann. "Introduction." In *On the Road*. Edited by Jack Kerouac. New York: Viking, 1958, ix–xxxii.

Danquah, J. B. *The Akan Doctrine of God: A Fragment of Gold Coast Ethics and Religion*. London: Frank Cass, 1944.

Davie, Donald. *Ezra Pound*. New York: Viking, 1975.

Dickinson, Emily. *The Complete Poems of Emily Dickinson*. Edited by Thomas H. Johnson. Boston: Little, Brown, 1960.

Durant, Alan. "Pound, Modernism and Literary Criticism: A Reply to Donald Davie." *Critical Quarterly* 28 (Spring-Summer 1986): 154–66.

Eliot, T. S. *Selected Essays, 1917–1932*. New York: Harcourt, 1932.

Ellison, Ralph. "Richard Wright's Blues." *Antioch Review* 5 (June 1945): 198–211.

———. *Shadow and Act*. New York: Random House, 1964.

Emanuel, James A. *Jazz from the Haiku King*. Detroit: Broadside, 1999.

Emerson, Ralph Waldo. *Selections from Ralf Waldo Emerson*. Edited by Stephen E. Whicher. Boston: Houghton Mifflin, 1960.

Fabre, Michel. *The Unfinished Quest of Richard Wright*. New York: Morrow, 1973.

———. "The Poetry of Richard Wright." In *Critical Essays of Richard Wright*. Edited by Yoshinobu Hakutani. Boston: G. K. Hall, 1975, 252–72.

————. *Richard Wright: Books and Writers*. Jackson: University Press of Mississippi, 1990.

Fenollosa, Ernest. *The Chinese Written Character as a Medium for Poetry*. Edited by Ezra Pound. New York: Arrow, 1936.

Frost, Robert. *Robert Frost's Poems*. Edited by Louis Untermeyer. New York: Pocket Books, 1971.

Gifford, Barry and Lawrence Lee. *Jack's Book: An Oral Biography of Jack Kerouac*. New York: St. Martin's, 1978.

Goodwin, K. L. *The Influence of Ezra Pound*. London: Oxford University Press, 1966.

Graham, Don B. "Yone Noguchi's 'Poe Mania.'" *Markham Review* 4 (1974): 58–60.

Haas, Robert. "Five Haiku by Richard Wright (Review)." *Washington Post*. April 11, 1999.

Hakutani, Yoshinobu. "Yone Noguchi's Poetry: From Whitman to Zen." *Comparative Literature Studies* 22 (1985): 67–79.

————. "Father and Son: A Conversation with Isamu Noguchi." *Journal of Modern Literature* 42 (Summer 1990): 13–33.

————. "Ezra Pound, Yone Noguchi, and Imagism." *Modern Philology* 90 (August 1992): 46–69.

————. *Richard Wright and Racial Discourse*. Columbia: University of Missouri Press, 1996.

————. "Richard Wright's Haiku, Zen, and the African 'Primal Outlook upon Life.'" *Modern Philology* 104 (May 2007): 510–28.

Harmer, J. B. *Victory in Limbo: Imagism 1908–1917*. New York: St. Martin's, 1975.

Henderson, Harold G. *An Introduction to Haiku: An Anthology of Poems and Poets from Basho to Shiki*. New York: Doubleday/Anchor, 1958.

Higginson, William. *The Haiku Handbook*. New York: McGraw-Hill, 1985.

Hughes, Langston. *Selected Poems of Langston Hughes*. New York: Knopf, 1959.

Imoto, Noichi. *Basho: Sono Jinsei to Geijitsu [Basho: His Life and Art]*. Tokyo: Kodansha, 1968.

Jefferson, Thomas. *Notes on the State of Virginia*. Edited by William Peden. Chapel Hill: University of North Carolina Press, 1955.

Jones, A. R. *The Life and Opinions of Thomas Ernest Hulme*. Boston: Beacon, 1960.

Jones, Gayl. *Liberating Voices: Oral Tradition in African-American Literature*. Cambridge: Harvard University Press, 1991.

Keene, Donald. *World within Walls: Japanese Literature of the Pre-Modern Era, 1600–1868*. New York: Grove, 1976.

Kenner, Hugh. *The Poetry of Ezra Pound*. Millwood, NY: Kraus, 1947.

Kerouac, Jack. "Essentials of Spontaneous Prose." *Evergreen Review* 2 (Summer 1958): 72–73.

————. *On the Road*. New York: Viking, 1957.

————. *The Dharma Bums*. New York: Viking, 1958.

————. *Book of Haikus*. Edited by Regina Weinreich. New York: Penguin Books, 2003.

Kiuchi, Toru. "On Sinclair Beiles," *Letter to Yoshinobu Hakutani*, August 7, 2005.

Kodama, Sanehide. ed. *Ezra Pound and Japan: Letters and Essays*. Redding Ridge, CT: Black Swan Books, 1987.

Kurebayashi, Kodo. *Introduction to Dogen Zen* [in Japanese]. Tokyo: Daihorinkaku, 1983.

Lacan, Jacques. *The Four Fundamental of Concepts of Psychoanalysis*. Edited by Jacques-Alain Miller. Translated by Alan Sheridan. New York: Norton, 1881.

———. *The Seminar of Jacques Lacan*, bk. 2, *The Ego in Freud's Theory and in the Techniques of Psychoanalysis, 1954–1955*. Edited by Jacques-Alain Miller and Translated by Sylvana Tomaselli. New York: Norton, 1988.

Lewitz, Leza. "Richard Wright's Haiku (Review)." *Japan Times*. April 27, 1999.

Loehr, Max. *The Great Paintings of China*. New York: Harper and Row, 1980.

Lynch, Tom. "Intersecting Influences in American Haiku." In *Modernity in East-West Literary Criticism: New Readings*. Edited by Yoshinobu Hakutani. Madison: Fairleigh Dickinson University Press, 2001.

McMichael, George, et al. *Anthology of American Literature* II, 8th ed. Upper Saddle River, NJ: Prentice Hall, 2004.

Melville, Herman. *Moby-Dick*. Edited by Harrison Hayford and Hershel Parker. New York: Norton, 1967.

Miller, Liam. *The Noble Drama of W. B. Yeats*. Dublin: Dolmen, 1977.

Miner, Earl. "Pound, Haiku and the Image." *Hudson Review* 9 (Winter 1957): 570–84.

———. *The Japanese Tradition in British and American Literature*. Princeton: Princeton University Press, 1958.

Morrison, Toni. *Jazz*. New York: Plume, 1993.

Noguchi, Isamu. *A Sculptor's World*. New York: Harper & Row, 1968.

Noguchi, Yone. *Seen and Unseen*. San Francisco: Burgess & Garnett, 1897.

———. *The Voice of the Valley*. San Francisco: Doxey, 1897.

———. *The American Diary of a Japanese Girl*. New York: Frank Leslie Publishing House, 1901.

———. *From the Eastern Sea*. London: Elkin Mathews, 1903.

———. *The Summer Cloud: Prose Poems*. Tokyo: Shunyodo, 1906.

———. *The Pilgrimage*. 2 vols. Tokyo: Kyobunkan, 1909.

———. *Kamakura*. Kamakura: Valley, 1910.

———. "Koyetsu." *Rhythm* 11, No. 11 (December 1912): 302–05.

———. "What Is a Hokku Poem?" *Rhythm* 11, No. 10 (January 1913): 354–59.

———. "Japanese Poetry." *The Transactions of the Japan Society of London* 12 (1914): 86–109.

———. "The Last Master [Yoshitoshi] of the Ukiyoye School." *The Transactions of the Japan Society of London* 12 (April 1914): 144–56.

———. *The Spirit of Japanese Poetry*. London: John Murray, 1914.

———. *The Story of Yone Noguchi Told by Himself*. London: Chatto and Windus, 1914.

———. *The Spirit of Japanese Art*. New York: Dutton, 1915.

———. "The Everlasting Sorrow: A Japanese Noh Play." *Egoist* 4 (1917): 141–43.

———. "The Japanese Noh Play." *Egoist* 5 (1918): 99.

———. *Japanese Hokkus*. Boston: Four Seas, 1920.

———. *Hiroshige*. London: Elkin Mathews, 1921.

———. *Japan and America*. Tokyo: Keio University Press, 1921.

———. *Korin*. London: Elkin Mathews, 1922.

————. *Through the Torii*. Boston: Four Seas, 1922.

————. *Utamaro*. London: Elkin Mathews, 1923.

————. *Hokusai*. London: Elkin Mathews, 1924.

————. *Harunobu*. London: Elkin Mathews, 1927.

————. *The Ukiyoye Primitives*. Tokyo: Privately published, 1933.

————. *Hiroshige and Japanese Landscapes*. Tokyo: Maruzen, 1936.

————. *Collected English Letters*. Edited by Ikuko Atsumi. Tokyo: Yone Noguchi Society, 1975.

————. *Selected English Writings of Yone Noguchi: An East-West Literary Assimilation*. Edited by Yoshinobu Hakutani. 2 vols. Rutherford, NJ: Fairleigh Dickinson University Press/London: Associated University Presses, 1990, 1992.

————. *The Diary of a Japanese Girl*. Edited with Original Illustrations by Genjiro Yeto. Philadelphia: Temple University Press, 2007.

Poe, Edgar Allan. *Selected Writings of Edgar Allan Poe*. Edited by Edward H. Davidson. Boston: Houghton Mifflin, 1956.

————. *The Complete Works of Edgar Allan Poe*. Edited by James Albert Harrison. New York: Crowell, 1902.

Pound, Ezra. "Vorticism." *Fortnightly Review,* No. 573, n. s. (1914): 461–71.

————. "As for Imagisme." *New Age* 14 (1915): 349.

————. *Gaudier-Brzeska: A Memoir*. New York: New Directions, 1916, 1970.

————. *Personae*. New York: New Directions, 1926.

————. *Literary Essays of Ezra Pound*. Edited and intro. T. S. Eliot. New York: New Directions, 1954.

————. *Ezra Pound: Selected Poems*. New York: New Directions, 1957.

————. *The Spirit of Romance*. New York: New Directions, 1968.

Pound, Ezra and Ernest Fenollosa. *The Classic Noh Theatre of Japan*. New York: New Directions, 1959.

Pratt, William. *The Imagist Poem*. New York: Dutton, 1963.

Sanchez, Sonia. *Like the Singing Coming off the Drums*. Boston: Beacon, 1998.

————. *Morning Haiku*. Boston: Beacon, 2010.

Sharp, E. A. *William Sharp: A Memoir*. London: Heinemann, 1910.

Shirane, Haruo. *Traces of Dreams: Lanscape, Cultural Memory, and the Poetry of Bashō*. Stanford, CA: Stanford University Press, 1998.

Snyder, Gary. "Translation of Shan Han's "Cold Mountain." *Anthology of American Literature*. Edited by George McMichael, et al. Glenview, IL: Longman, 2011. 1687.

Stepto, Robert. *From behind the Veil: A Study of Afro-American Narrative*. Urbana: University of Illinois Press, 1979.

Stock, Noel. *Poet in Exile: Ezra Pound*. Manchester: Manchester University Press, 1964.

Stoddard, Charles Warren. "Introduction." In *The Voice of the Valley*. Edited by Yone Noguchi. San Francisco; Doxey, 1897, 10–11.

Teele, Roy E. "The Japanese Translations." *Texas Quarterly* 10 (1967): 61–66.

Thoreau, Henry David. *The Variorum Civil Disobedience*. Edited by Walter Harding. New York: Twayne, 1967.

————. *Walden.* Edited by J. Lyndon Shanley. Princeton, NJ: Princeton University Press, 1971.

————. *A Week on the Concord and Merrimack Rivers.* Edited by Carl F. Hovde, et al. Princeton, NJ: Princeton University Press, 1980.

Tonkinson, Carol, ed. *Big Sky Mind: Buddhism and the Beat Gerneration.* New York: Riverhead, 1995.

Toyama, Usaburo, ed. *Essays on Yone Noguchi.* 3 vols. Tokyo: Zokei Bijutsu Kyokai, 1963.

Twain, Mark. *Adventures of Huckleberry Finn.* Edited by Sculley Bradley et al. New York: Norton, 1977.

Tytell, John. *Naked Angels: The Lives & Literature of the Beat Generation.* New York: McGraw-Hill, 1977.

Ueda, Makoto. *Zeami, Basho, Yeats, Pound: A Study in Japanese and English Poetics.* The Hague: Mouton, 1965.

Waley, Arthur. *The Nō Plays of Japan.* New York: Grove, 1920.

Walker, Margaret. *Richard Wright: Daemonic Genius.* New York: Warner Books, 1988.

Webb, Constance. *Richard Wright: A Biography.* New York: Putnam, 1968.

Werner, Craig. *Playing the Changes: From Afro-Modernism to the Jazz Impulse.* Urbana: University of Illinois Press, 1994.

————. *A Change Is Gonna Come: Music, Race & the Soul of America.* New York: Plume, 1999.

Whitman, Walt. *Complete Poetry and Selected Prose.* Edited by James E. Miller, Jr. Boston: Houghton Mifflin, 1959.

————. *Leaves of Grass.* Edited by Sculley Bradley, et al. New York: New York University Press, 1980.

Wright, Julia. "Introduction." In *Haiku: This Other World.* Edited by Richard Wright, Yoshinobu Hakutani, and Robert L. Tener. New York: Arcade, 1998. Rpt. New York: Random House, 2000, vii–xii.

Wright, Richard. *12 Million Black Voices: A Folk History of the Negro in the United States.* New York: Viking, 1941.

————. *Black Power: A Record of Reactions in a Land of Pathos.* New York: Harper, 1954.

————. *Pagan Spain.* New York: Harper and Brothers, 1957.

————. *Four Thousand Haiku.* New Haven, CT: Beinecke Rare Book and Manuscript Library, Yale University, 1960.

————. This Other World: Projections in the Haiku Manner. New Haven: Beinecke Rare Book and Manuscript Library, Yale University, 1960.

————. "Blueprint for Negro Writing." In *Richard Wright Reader.* Edited by Ellen Wright and Michel Fabre. New York: Harper, 1978, 36–49.

————. *Conversations with Richard Wright.* Edited by Keneth Kinnamon and Michel Fabre. Jackson: University Press of Mississippi, 1993.

————. *Native Son.* 1940. New York: Harper and Row, 1966.

————. *Haiku: This Other World.* Edited by Yoshinobu Hakutani and Robert L. Tener. New York: Arcade, 1998. Rpt. New York: Random House, 2000.

Yasuda, Kenneth. *A Pepper-Rod: A Haiku Sampler*. Rutland, VT: Charles Tuttle, 1957.

———. *The Japanese Haiku*. Rutland, VT: Charles Tuttle, 1957.

Yeats, W. B. *Reveries over Childhood and Youth*. Dublin: Cuala, 1916.

———. *Autobiography*. New York: Macmillan, 1938.

———. "Introduction to Certain Noble Plays of Japan by Pound & Fenollosa." In *The Classic Noh Theatre of Japan*. New York: New Directions, 1959, 151–63.

———. *The Variorum Edition of the Plays of W. B. Yeats*. Edited by Russell K. Alspach. New York: Macmillan, 1966.

———. *The Poems of W. B. Yeats*. Edited by Richard J. Finneran. New York: Macmillan, 1983.

Youmans, Rich. "For My Wife on Our First Anniversary." *Brussels Sprout* 11, No. 3 (1994): 15.

Index of Haiku and Poems

Subject Index

About the Author

Yoshinobu Hakutani is Professor of English and University Distinguished Scholar at Kent State University in Ohio. He is the author of several recent books, including *East-West Literary Imagination: Cultural Exchanges from Yeats to Morrison* (2017), *Richard Wright and Haiku* (2014), *Haiku and Modernist Poetics* (2009), and *Cross-Cultural Visions in African American Modernism: From Spatial Narrative to Jazz Haiku* (2006).

Lightning Source UK Ltd.
Milton Keynes UK
UKHW040721310319
340208UK00006B/134/P